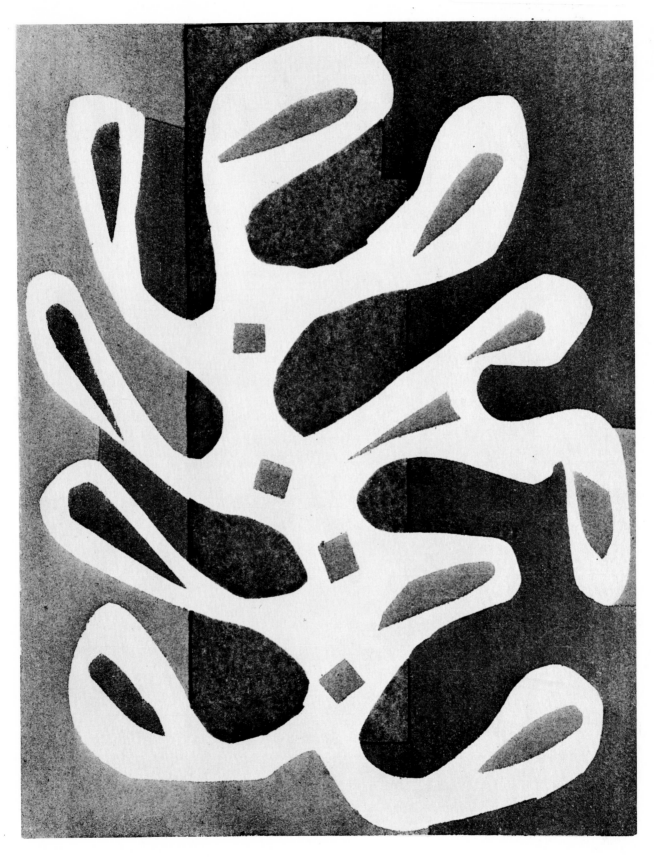

PAPER CUTOUT BY MATISSE

creating

SEATTLE & LONDON

with paper

BASIC FORMS AND VARIATIONS

By PAULINE JOHNSON

UNIVERSITY OF WASHINGTON PRESS

Copyright © 1958 by the University of Washington Press
Second printing, 1958
Third printing, 1959
Fourth and fifth printings, 1960
Sixth printing, 1961
Seventh printing, 1962
Eighth printing, 1963
Ninth printing, 1965
Tenth printing, 1966
Eleventh printing, 1967
Twelfth printing, 1969
Thirteenth printing, 1971
Fourteenth printing, 1973
Paperback edition, 1975
Second printing (paper), 1981
Library of Congress Catalog Card Number 58-6007
ISBN (paper) 0-295-95408-6
Printed in the United States of America

The techniques described in this book are for using paper
as a creative art medium for educational and noncommercial
purposes. Any person contemplating commercial application is
cautioned that such use may be subject to existing patent rights.

FOREWORD

These words might have been graven in stone with a chisel or inscribed with a quill on vellum or scratched with a crayon on slate. In fact, they were written with a pen on paper, and appropriately so since they are the outcome of thoughts inspired by Pauline Johnson's book on the art of working with paper. Reading the text had two effects that are indicative of its character. It set me thinking of experiences I had thought long forgotten, and it made me seek out a pair of scissors and a rule so that I might at once try out some of the things she describes. In this way I realized anew how responsive a medium this everyday material paper can be.

One of the great basic inventions of mankind, as important for the growth of civilization as the discovery of the wheel or the firing of glass, paper is a fabulous material, diverse in qualities and adaptable in use. Rough and smooth, delicate and strong, prized and despised—on it Shakespeare wrote sonnets and Dürer drew praying hands, while the fishmonger wraps cod in it for which the housewife will pay in paper currency. In the Welsh village where I was born, because they were poor, the men used to have special suits for funerals made of a shiny, carbon-black paper like the end papers in their nonconformist hymnbooks.

Much of the remembered excitement and mystery of Christmas remains associated with paper. Apart from the colored fans and the chains suspended from corner to corner of the dining room, those misshapen bulging stockings hanging at the foot of the bed in the early half-light of Christmas morning had an even more intriguing fascination when they crackled as we lifted them down. Somewhere inside there would be a little star-shaped Japanese paper fan with magenta or emerald sticks that could be twisted around inside out to look like a small, exotic parakeet. Almost invariably, there would be as well one package with dozens of different colored papers in layers, like Chinese carved ivory puzzles, which would reveal, after all the effort of unwrapping, only a walnut or some trifling thing. The section devoted to Christmas in this book introduces a range of suggestions appropriate to the season, imaginative designs that can be developed according to individual fancy and which, in the making, will afford a wealth of pleasure and satisfaction never obtainable from things purchased ready-made.

There was one man who, performing what for him were merely daily routine tasks, implanted in me an awesome respect for skill, a feeling for the potentialities of paper, and an as yet unconscious urge to shape and mold things creatively nearer to an inward desire. He was the village grocer. In my eyes, his supreme accomplishment was the mastery with which he weighed and wrapped the products he purveyed. Standing before the glinting brass scales, he would tip candies from a glass jar and then, without even turning round, would reach for one of the squares of paper already cut and stacked on the shelf behind him. With a quick flip, he would turn it from corner to corner around his right hand to form a cone, at the same time twisting the tip of the cone with his left, all as it were in one flowing movement.

Best of all was his performance with tea or rice or coffee. Tea went into a square of printed white paper, rice into one of soft blue paper that I preferred. Coffee not only had to be roasted, ground, and weighed, but was packed in *two* sheets of paper, a shiny brown kind outside and an opaque, white, grease-proof kind inside. Almost fastidiously, the grocer would bring the edges of paper together and fold them over twice into a flat pleat. Passing his fingers and thumbs caressingly up and down the coffee-filled cylinder, he would shape it and fold over the ends of the papers, tucking in the triangular corner and finally tying the rounded parallelogram with fine white twine.

Many years later I was faced with the problems of designing scenery and costumes for an enthusiastic but impoverished little theater group. The seeds of impressions stored up in childhood came to my aid, and, now transfigured through conscious adult esthetic awareness and strengthened by the boldness of forms studied in primitive art, they emerged as masks and head-dresses created from colored construction paper. After some experiments with techniques, I found that the limits of the extent to which the material could be manipulated, beyond which it lost resilience and crispness, determined the nature of the designs and were favorable to simplification and abstraction.

During World War II, I came into contact with one of the great traditions of paper craft. In the art gallery in the United Kingdom of which I was then director, we had arranged an exhibition of paintings by expatriate, refugee Polish soldiers. One of them prepared for the entrance to the exhibition a decorative arch that included the Polish arms and eagles, all solidly represented as if carved in white plaster. In fact they were intricately constructed of paper, and for me there was special interest in comparing the technique of building up numerous small items to a monumental whole with the one I had evolved, independently of a direct folk tradition, of folding or creasing into large areas of paper the modeling required to meet theatrical conditions.

There are innumerable examples of folk traditions that have survived in paper craft or have become the sources for further artistic experiment. In London, and maybe elsewhere, there are entertainers known as "buskers," latter-day troubadours or jongleurs, who sing, recite, dance, and tumble for the diversion of people waiting in queues outside theaters. Among the more popular of these artists are men who pleat and tear newspapers, unfolding them to reveal a string of dancers or elaborately pierced doilies. The climax to the act usually comes when one of them rolls, twists, and tears a newspaper, building up excitement with pantomime and asides before giving the paper a final rap on his leg and then slowly pushing it up, extending what proves to be a Jacob's ladder. Higher and higher skyward it goes — thin tubes at each side with slats at intervals across and a gingerbread man on the top. Then some wayward gust of wind catches the frail structure; it quivers, teeters, and comes crashing down.

In Mexico and Japan, perhaps more than in any other countries, paper has been elaborated into the pattern of culture. It may be that their backgrounds of exceptional sources of natural disaster, which take heavy toll of lives lightly valued, are conducive to the elaboration of art forms symbolically frail and ephemeral, explosive and transitory—paper toys and lanterns, firecrackers, and friable pottery. Watching those swarms of lighted lanterns floating in the night at festival time down rivers or streams in Japan, or seeing those long-limbed Mexican paper figures explode in the air, induces an intuitive feeling of something both futile and sublime, an "otherliness" or symbolic nonattachment that comes near to an ecstatic catharsis, akin to the dying fall implicit in the leap of a dancer, and carrying within it the pathos of a grief. Their inherent oppositions of fire and water, earth and air, rising and falling are esthetic or poetic images of the condition of man.

In Tokyo I saw, with immense delight, large displays of pleated and colored paper fans, flowers, and wreaths piled up elaborately outside new stores before they were to be opened. Meretricious and even garish in detail, they made a splendid array in the mass. The pleasure of receiving a gift was greatly heightened by the elegant charm of the wrapping, with a triangular-folded message or greeting tucked into the corner of the package. I cannot forget visiting a small shop in a narrow street where all the members of the family, squatting on the floor, were pasting silky textured paper over coils of cane to make variously shaped lanterns. Some were freshly painted in brilliant red with bold black calligraphic characters to serve as shop signs, while others were shaped and painted to represent dolls. Next door, other artists were painting paper kites and long paper fishes. They were all engaged in making by hand items that would be sold for very little money, and it seemed incredible that these products of such skill and artistry would be treated as lightly expendable. On the other hand, in Kamakura there was a famous artist who spent his time exclusively in painting on paper lanterns and fans, each exquisite motif delineated with fine sensitivity, and these were regarded as rare treasures to be acquired by connoisseurs. At many of the temples I visited, there were prayer trees with small strips of prayer-inscribed paper twisted on each small branch and twig. Delicately they fluttered like living snow, with a faint rustle as if the suppliants were aware that wishes and desires and life and death are subject to the chances of winds that blow.

In this book, Pauline Johnson deals with a large area of the world of paper, less concerned with its mundane utility for wrapping and conveying messages than with its uses as a medium serving the needs of art and the ends of education. From this point of view, what distinguishes the book is the planned development of the whole and of the separate sections. The educational and artistic intentions are never consciously separated. In giving specific examples of how to pleat or fold different kinds ot paper for certain defined purposes, or even in describing the varieties of paper that can be found, the author seems to aim at an exploratory and responsive approach, a freely creative and inherently evolving attitude. From my experiences as Programme Specialist for Education through the Arts and Crafts at the United Nations Educational Scientific and Cultural Organization in Paris, I know there is a real need for craft manuals that not only set a high standard of design but also inculcate modes of teaching and learning that will preserve the germinal seeds of creative inspiration, so that neither the practice nor the product of art will become stereotyped but will contain within themselves an evolutionary vitality. Books of this kind will meet not only the textbook requirements of advanced institutions in countries like the United States, but also, and maybe more essentially, the needs of general schools and art colleges in those countries which are in process of revising, developing, and even for the first time initiating their educational programs. For such as these, a book dealing with a craft that requires inexpensive materials and little basic equipment will offer an ideal solution to many problems.

This is not the first book to be written about the art of paper folding and modeling, but it is one of the best from an educational point of view, and it offers a wide range of techniques and ideas that will appeal to various people according to their needs. Those who are already experts will appreciate having so much information and such a wealth of illustrative examples conveniently assembled. For students it will be an essential textbook describing basic techniques and providing high standards of design. Classroom teachers will find it an invaluable source of inspiration and a sure guide to sound principles of educational practice. Those who are responsible for planning activities for youth organizations often express the need for guidance as to arts and crafts projects, and this book offers an immensely rewarding resource for this purpose.

Apart from its value in these ways as a manual for educational institutions, it will have a wider appeal to those generally interested in leisure-time activities. The steadily increasing numbers of people who seek a means of focusing their urge to express themselves through creative forms of art or craft, but who may be timid about embarking on anything that appears to be technically too difficult or too costly, may well find that paper craft offers a simple but unending source of personal enrichment and satisfaction. For this ephemeral and eternal material, vehicle for the greatest art and the finest poetry, for lovers' vows and nations' treaties, daily discarded and preciously preserved, impressed and printed, folded and molded, pulped and crumpled, twisted and turned, packed and wrapped, can be used in an infinite variety of ways, daily serving utilitarian purposes and eternally employed as the medium of creative expression.

Trevor Thomas

PREFACE

Paper is a wonderfully inspiring material, challenging to the imagination, vital as a medium for man's expressive purposes, yet essential for serving a vast amount of the world's utilitarian needs. Its importance as a vehicle for communication is evident, since it is a basic medium for transmitting news and information, thoughts and ideas, through letters, circulars, books, periodicals, and newspapers. Once the principle of printing with movable blocks had been discovered, the whole horizon of the dissemination of knowledge was enlarged, and with it the utilization of paper as the basic material to receive the imprint of words of historical importance and literary value. It is the means for conveying the message contained in this book, serving to transmit both written and pictorial elements.

In many communities of the world, paper has become an essential part of the cultural pattern and a source of artistic enrichment within local traditions. The paper cutouts of Poland, for instance, renowned for their vitality and expressiveness, have long been recognized as a folk art. In Mexico, paper is an important part of many festivals in which banners, *piñatas*, and various other structures are used in elaborate spectacles. It is remarkable to find in all of these arts of the people an underlying good taste and an appreciation of the expressive qualities of paper. A sensitivity for harmonious relations of shapes and ornament is revealed, with inspired creations growing out of real feeling produced by culture and environment.

In Japan, for various reasons, partly traditional, partly arising out of the climate, the environment, and economic necessity, paper is used for many utilitarian purposes. This functional expediency in the use of a relatively inexpensive and readily available material, when acted upon by the innate sensibility of the Japanese people, has resulted in a variety of things which, though ephemeral, are often artful and amusing. Paper folding is a favorite pastime for both children and adults in Japan, and yet it is important enough to be recognized as an art for exhibition.

Paper art has flourished in many other countries. The making of silhouettes, for example, was once an art sponsored in convents throughout Europe. Painters have found paper useful for cutting shapes to be studied and related as they plan the composition of their pictures. Henri Matisse devoted his later years to making flat cutout paper shapes that are comparable in vitality to his paintings. These he utilized as the basis for church decorations, stained glass, vestments, and other designs.

This book is planned from the point of view of using paper in the production of art forms, and is devoted to seeing and thinking of paper as a medium for artistic expression. The focus of attention is upon esthetic values, with emphasis upon abstract qualities. A progressive summary of working with paper is given through a visual presentation of contour, plane, volume, and space in two- and three-dimensional forms.

Treated flat, paper results in an "art of the surface" in which rhythmic intervals and contrasts of values are revealed in cut areas. When modeled, or three-dimensional, it becomes sculptural, resulting in an "art of volume," of form in space. Since the ultimate aim is pure form, the expression must grow out of regard for the material as such, and for the restrictions it imposes. An awareness of nature as a part of environmental influence contributes to impressions and to inspiration. Nature, however, is only a source, and not to be imitated as an end in itself.

The creation of art is the creation of true vitality, and the controlling factor in arriving at standards of judgment is design. Growing out of a living concept of art, acquaintance with the principles of design makes possible an understanding and appreciation of quality wherever found—old or new, from a museum or a commercial source, from a ten-cent store or an expensive shop. Some regard only the art of the present as having value, but excellent sources for contemporary design can be found in our own past as well as in other cultures. A constantly growing sensitivity to everything we come into contact with is necessary in order to encourage good design and improve standards of taste. Only in a climate conducive to the natural development of exploration and experimentation can real growth take place. Such development cannot be forced into a plan of formalized procedure. The worker must be permitted to sense the excitement of the material and have an opportunity to respond to it intuitively. His response will reflect unfolding tastes, talents, and power of invention.

Education should provide opportunities for the creative impulses of all to find expression through suitable materials. The types of experiences presented in this book are adaptable to almost any age level—the complexity of decorative surface design and the intellectual handling of intricate form relationships are the major factors that will vary with age and understanding. Development should be a matter of continuing awareness and exploration of the world of the imagination, guided always by the principles of good design.

This book was originally intended as a manual for the use of students and teachers, presenting various approaches for working with paper as a creative art medium. It might have remained limited in scope had not the interest of friends and colleagues prompted a more thorough and extensive treatment of the subject. A grant was subsequently obtained from the Agnes H. Anderson Research Fund of the University of Washington, making it possible to enlarge the initial undertaking and secure the assistance of Hazel Koenig and Aileen Moseley. These talented artists, both teachers in the children's creative art classes at the University of Washington, caught the spirit of the production and cooperated enthusiastically in contributing their abilities. Many of the models used in the photographs were designed and constructed by them expressly for this publication. Their loyal support and belief in the project were perhaps the most decisive factors in determining the extent to which it was finally carried. They also found that the experience of participating in the research necessary to study the limitations of the materials and discover solutions for technical problems provided an opportunity for the growth of imaginative resources. This has proved to be a valuable asset in teaching effectiveness—evidence that the approach here presented is basically sound and creative.

Trevor Thomas, British art educator formerly with UNESCO in Paris, read parts of the manuscript and contributed valuable suggestions, in addition to preparing a Foreword that serves to set a mood for the book. His interest and encouragement, stemming from personal experience with this fascinating medium, are greatly appreciated.

Since the ideas presented here rely heavily upon the use of photographs to show the pattern and form qualities of the structures, it was important to secure clarity by strong contrasts, and subtle modulations by controlled lighting. Recognition is given to the Still Photography Production Unit of the University of Washington where all the photographs, except as indicated, were produced under the direction of E. F. Marten, who cooperated fully in meeting the compositional and technical requirements necessary to achieve the desired results.

Thanks are expressed to H. O. Gummerus, managing director of the Arts and Crafts and Industrial Design School of Helsinki, for graciously contributing the photographs on pages 9 and 52; to André Lejard of Les Editions du Chêne, publisher of *Sculptures de Picasso,* for permission to reproduce the photograph by Brassaï of the Picasso structure; to Heinz Berggruen of Berggruen & Cie. for permission to use the paper cutout by Matisse; to Wendell Brazeau for the photograph in figure 7, page 73; to Peter Stone for the photograph on page 142; and to O. M. Hartsell for obtaining the photograph in figure 5, page 155.

The photograph on page 166 is reproduced by courtesy of Underwood & Underwood News Photos, Inc.; the photograph on page 206 by courtesy of the American Crayon Company, photographer James H. Reed. The following three photographs are reproduced by courtesy of *Life* Magazine: page 143, © 1954 Time Inc.; figure 6, page 153, © 1956 Time Inc.; page 154, © 1950 Time Inc.

Several of the examples used in the book were generously contributed by friends and students, to whom thanks is also extended. It is hoped they will enjoy seeing evidence of the part they had in the forming of this production. Others gave assistance through advice and encouragement and in various ways. Special acknowledgment is given to Jerry Conrad, Lydia Goos, Marvin Herard, Don Normark, and Mildred Sherwood for their important contributions toward the completion of the manuscript.

Pauline Johnson

STRUCTURE OF CARDBOARD STRIPS

CONTENTS

CARDBOARD STRUCTURE BY PICASSO

creating with paper

BASIC FORMS AND VARIATIONS

MATERIALS AND TOOLS

PAPERS

    Newsprint; bond and mimeograph papers
    A roll of butcher or Kraft paper
    Construction paper, white and colored
    Colored poster paper and coated papers
    Drawing paper with sized surface
    Water-color paper; engineer's drawing detail paper
    Metallic paper; crepe paper; parchment
    Tissue paper; tracing paper; cellophane
    Oatmeal paper and Textone
    Bristol board and tag board
    Chipboard for constructions, and as a cutting surface

CUTTERS

    Scissors—average size, and small manicure type for intricate cutting
    Sharp-pointed stencil knife
    Razor blade or mat cutter
    Dull kitchen knife

RULERS

    Straight ruler with metal edge
    Metal square

ADHESIVES

    Transparent tape; masking tape; double-coated tape
    Library paste; rubber cement; milky rubber-base glue

FASTENERS

    Staplers—small, average, and extra long
    Spring clothespins to hold paper during construction
    Metal brads; wire paper clips; eyelets; pins

MISCELLANEOUS

    Punch; compass; eraser

INTRODUCTION TO PAPER

There are a great many different kinds of paper. Each has its own distinguishing characteristics arising from its organic structure and revealed in its texture, translucence, and tensile strength, and these qualities serve to identify and distinguish one from the other. Thus, paper can be rough, smooth, transparent, opaque, thin, heavy, fine, tough, or fragile.

Some papers can be found quite readily in ordinary everyday use; for others of a more specialized nature, it may be necessary to search in out-of-the-way places, using imagination as to their possibilities from the artistic point of view. Thus, the papers shown in the photographs on the facing page are normally used for other than artistic purposes. The paper at the bottom was found in a butcher's shop, where it had been put through a cubing machine that is used to roughen the surface of meats. The paper was treated in this way in order to make it more absorbent, but from our point of view the roughed-up surface has an attractive textural quality that suggests all kinds of possibilities for imaginative use. This is but one example of how exciting and frequently rewarding an experience it can be to explore in unexpected places for materials, many of which can often be obtained at little or no cost. For instance, it may be well worth while making friendly contact with the local printing plant or bookbinding firm where, at the end of the day, the paper trimmings are thrown into waste bins. These are often quite varied in colors and kinds and are particularly good for the many uses where strips can be employed.

The type of paper known as newsprint is perhaps the least costly of any and can usually be obtained without much difficulty from a local newspaper office. Similarly, old newspapers can be especially useful for making experiments, since there are always plenty of them to be had, and there is no need to feel guilty about being wasteful or extravagant in using them lavishly. These are helpful in making paper patterns, such as those required when designing play or party costumes, in which much initial planning is essential and discarded trial designs have to be thrown away. For exploring or trying out various techniques in cutting and folding, typing, mimeograph, and bond papers are adequate and have the advantages of being responsive to handling, not too costly, and generally available. Another very serviceable paper for general utility is butcher or Kraft paper, which because of its strength and flexibility is excellent to use for all kinds of purposes. Shelf paper, commonly used at home, has a pleasant coated surface, can be folded easily, and, like all of the papers referred to here, is a responsive material with which to work.

Ready availability and low cost have been emphasized not so much for the sake of cheapness in itself but because these two factors make it possible for anyone to try out this fascinating art and for teachers to initiate it with their pupils within the limits of restricted budgets. They can do so without feeling obliged to undertake a heavy investment in equipment and materials and, more important, without feeling initially inhibited by any fear of wasting materials or of being unable to handle them.

Thus, with the simplest of materials, sufficient imagination, and a sensitive feeling for quality, satisfying results can be produced. Some of the most imaginative work has been created by world-famous artists employing the simplest materials, as can be seen in the photograph of the cardboard construction by Picasso. There are also more elaborate kinds of paper—papers with silk or other fibers embedded in them; or papers embossed with surface designs; or papers coated with various substances, like gold and silver metallic papers and glossy-surfaced drawing and printing card.

When white papers and cards are used in paper craft they are especially effective in helping to reveal sculptural form because light reflected from their monochrome surfaces creates subtle gradations of tone that emphasize the abstract features of the structural design. There are a number of varieties of papers and thin boards in this category, such as Bristol board, engineer's drawing detail paper, and parchment. Most schools are provided with or can secure white construction and drawing papers of various weights and qualities, obtainable either as single sheets or made up into tear-off pads. For the purposes of paper craft each of these has qualities that can be exploited in order to give folded edges with softer or sharper definition and with greater or lesser degrees of light reflection. Although the differences may be very subtle, familiarity and experience in the use of these various papers will enable the artist to employ whichever best suits his purpose.

There are times when a monochrome effect is desirable and stronger than a number of colors used together. Combinations of black with gray or white are often pleasing, making possible wide or subtle value contrasts depending upon the juxtaposition of the papers. An example is the silhouette—at one time a very popular art that flourished quite generally in Europe—in which the whole effect depends upon the contrast of dark with light.

Working with color brings in a different element of visual pleasure, not only in the color itself but in the various combinations possible, the value relationships of contrasting and distinguishing between colors, and the use of zones of colors in a composition to define specific areas. Papers suitable for use in this connection vary from light to heavy depending upon need. Poster and construction papers, most frequently used in schools, as well as colored glazed papers, gift wrappings, Japanese papers, and Bristol boards can all be explored for their chromatic as well as their plastic values. Blotting paper is now manufactured in a wide range of colors and was, in fact, one of the papers most frequently used in the early days of experiments with paper craft.

The senses of sight and touch respond in various ways to the texture or surface qualities of papers. Translucent examples like tissue paper, tracing paper, wax paper, cellophane, and onionskin, which have a light and airy feeling, are delightful to use where thinness and lucidity are desired. On the other hand, there may be projected a design in which the main interest or flavor will depend upon a feeling of strong textural quality in the material. In this event Textone, oatmeal, cream manila, crepe, and similar papers which are rough in "feel" will be ideal for the purpose. Again, an imaginative designer will soon appreciate the vitality and "aliveness" that can be imparted by sensitive combinations and contrasts of varying textures that in their associations serve to create richness of surface.

Both strength and delicacy are factors in the creation of paper art. There are times when actual structural strength is required so that the paper will be tough enough to resist considerable pull or tension, or thick enough to stand up of its own accord or to support the weight of some other feature. Typical examples of items in this category are oak tag, Bristol board, chipboard, and matting and illustration boards. Manufacturers produce hundreds of varieties of these, differently classified according to their surfaces, thicknesses, and composition, all offering many possibilities for use in the hands of creative artists. Sometimes strength is added to the paper pulp during manufacture by backing it with, or incorporating into it, some other element like chopped straw, muslin, or wire mesh. In the papers known as "plies," several layers are bonded together on the plywood principle, so that the lines of stress are set at different angles to each other and thus both tensile and structural strength are increased.

Among the best known and most frequently used of the papers and boards manufactured primarily for their strength are those which are corrugated. Sometimes the corrugations are left free so that the paper can be turned and rolled; otherwise they are backed by, or sandwiched between, layers of paper so that they are less flexible or even rigid. This principle of imparting strength to a flexible material by corrugating, folding, or pleating it (so excellently illustrated in the ruff, the concertina, and the diaphragm of a camera) is one universally employed and is the underlying structural feature of many of the examples illustrated in this book.

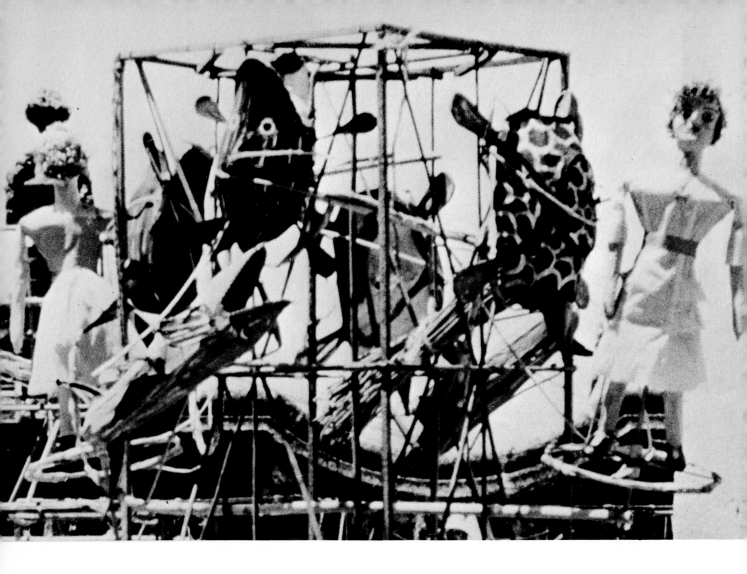

This wooden tower, called a castillo, is rigged with fireworks and used for religious festivals in Mexico. The paper structures are built over simple light reed armatures.

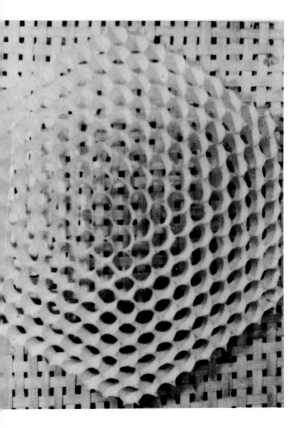

Paper is such a familiar item in our environment that it can all too easily be taken for granted. Yet before 200 B.C. no such product existed. Originally the Chinese were responsible for developing this material, which was introduced into Europe one thousand years later by the Arabs. In the nineteenth century the French scientist Réaumur observed a wasp taking slivers and bits of wood, chewing them into a pulp, and laying them in strips to make a nest. From this he conceived the idea of the mechanical disintegration of wood out of which came the basis of the wood pulp industry.

Paper is made from such constituents as wood pulp, vegetable fibers, rags, or a combination of these, which are chemically treated, beaten, mixed with water, and finally pressed. It is interesting to note the divergence of products that result from this process—newsprint, tissue, cardboard, in fact, up to several thousand different kinds of papers, each with distinguishing characteristics and many subtle variations.

Before paper became so plentiful it was respected as something precious and rare; now vast quantities are available, and it is an indispensable part of our lives. The demands for it have increased tremendously, and the production of paper has become so important that it is now the nation's fifth largest industry.

Every day we come into contact with a wide range of products made from paper, including such varied items as the morning newspaper, periodicals, books, facial tissues, packaged goods, and, of course, paper money. It is a significant characteristic of our society that we waste a great deal of this material. In fact, an important part of the industry is devoted to the production of disposable paper articles like cups, plates, napkins, and towels.

It is hoped that students and others will be made more aware of paper and its potentialities by experiencing and exploring the many possibilities it provides, guided by taste and the principles of design. A greater and more sensitive use of this material both for educational and for pleasurable purposes could make a real contribution to our culture.

A paper study from the Arts and Crafts and Industrial Design School of Helsinki, Finland (product design class; Ilmari Tapiovaara, adviser).

USES
FOR
PAPER

Many utilitarian objects made of paper have a beautiful sculptural form in their modeled structures. Making use of such geometric shapes as the sphere, the cube, and the cylinder, they are pleasing esthetically yet satisfactorily serve practical and industrial needs. The fluting on the cake cup and the fringe on the folded edges of the lamb frills are interesting details in the treatment of the paper. The relationship of the horizontal planes built into the vertical structure of the egg carton results in a form that is architectonic in construction. The form of the volume in the collapsible light shade has been controlled in accordance with the dimensions and the scoring of the folds.

An understanding of the limitations and special characteristics of paper is important in using it to the fullest advantage. Functional qualities like strength, lightness, transparency, toughness, smoothness, and other distinguishing factors must be considered in determining the kind of paper needed to solve each problem.

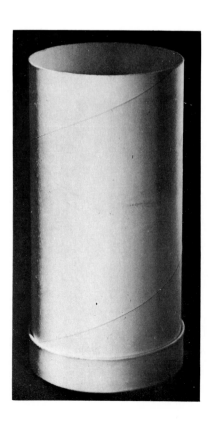

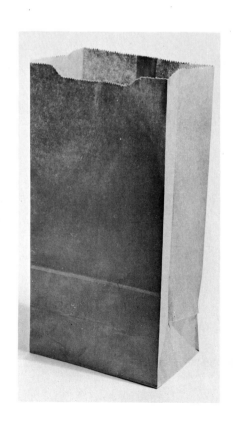

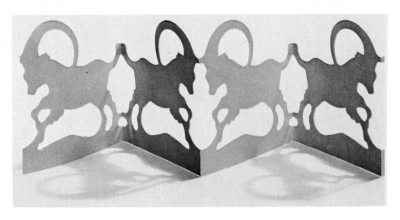

Paper has been an important means for carrying over tradition in festivals and religious ceremonies in many countries of the world. Some of the structures produced by other cultures have become familiar to us and are commonly accepted within our own. Although basically simple and geometric in form, they have modifications that help support their purpose and at the same time reveal interesting and varied treatments of the paper. For example, there are the ball with the honeycomb structure of thin paper sections which is designed to open and close, the party favor with gaily fringed ends, and the Japanese lantern enhanced by the functional concertina ridges on its surface. Some of the forms are derived from nature, like the Japanese fish kite, which becomes a modified cylinder when filled with air as it floats in the breeze. The ram in the multiple-fold cut and the star shape in the lantern constructed of three-sided points are traditional Swedish Christmas motifs.

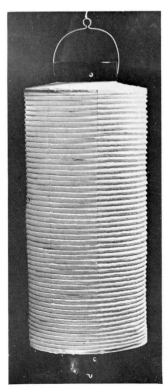

AN APPROACH TO FORM

The sculptural qualities of paper can be observed when a flat sheet is creased, rounded, or pleated to produce three-dimensional form. It then becomes a structure composed of alternating projected convex and concave surfaces which can be sensed visually or by touch, defined by modulations of dark and light values on the various sides. Controlled lighting produces shadows that help intensify the formal qualities, often with dramatic results.

When a lightweight piece of paper (preferably white) is crushed firmly within the hands, a consciousness of form qualities can be grasped as the bulky mass is handled and observed. When the crumpled paper is opened up, and a number of the folds formed by the crushing are emphasized, the paper will stand up like mountain peaks. Each of the flat surfaces produced by the creased edges is called a plane, an essential component also of painting, sculpture, and architecture.

It is well in studying the crushed structure to turn it around in your hands and look at it from all positions, noting the variations of line movement and rhythm. In this way, you will be made more aware of the meaning of abstract qualities and will become more sensitive to the recognition of art values wherever they are found.

Thus, nature can be seen as source and inspiration for creative work rather than something to be copied or imitated. This point of view helps discourage the use of stereotyped subject matter and the production of things which are trite or cute. In paper design it is important to retain an honesty and a paper-like feeling in the creations. Esthetic pleasure can then be found in the expressive values of the paper itself.

A modeled structure can be created by starting with a sheet of paper from which a section has been cut.

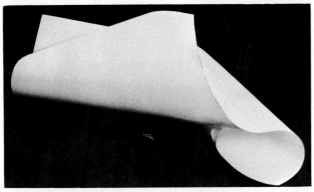

The paper can be rolled in various directions until a pleasing form is achieved. This can be held in position with tape or staples.

For another approach, the paper can be cut several times from the outer edges but retained all in one piece.

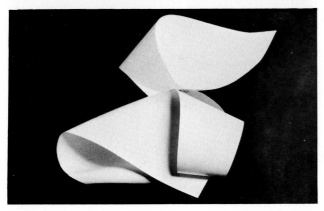

When the cut edges are lifted and rolled in different ways, a variety of forms can be created.

CUTTING

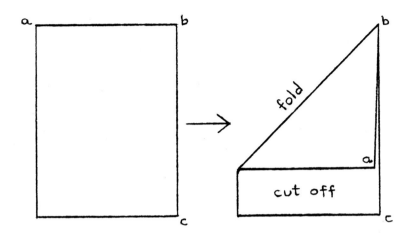

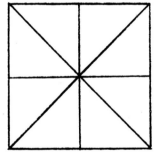

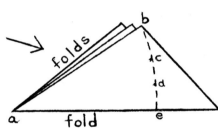

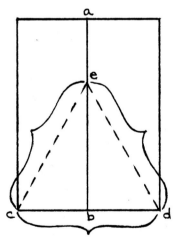

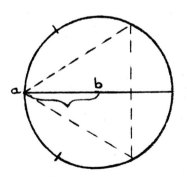

CUTTING A SQUARE

Bring side *ab* of a rectangle over to side *bc* and cut off extra piece below.

CUTTING A CIRCLE

Fold a square in half on the diagonal, forming a triangle. Fold in half again, and then in half again. Using *ab* as a measure, mark *ac*, *ad*, and *ae* and cut a connecting arc.

CUTTING A TRIANGLE

For an equilateral triangle, fold a rectangle in the center to get line *ab*. Draw a line *ce* the same length as *cd* and connect points *ed*. Or take the radius of a circle, *ab*, and mark off six times around the circumference. Connect every other point.

EXPANDING

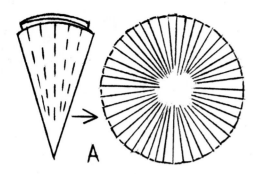

Fold a circle and cut fringe.

When cut in certain ways, paper can be stretched and expanded into new and different shapes. A circle folded and cut toward the center will fall into a fringed shape, varied according to the width of the strips and the weight of paper used. A shape cut by following the contour from the outside edge toward the center will automatically be extended into a long form (diagrams B and C). For the plan in diagram D, a square or rectangle is folded and cut alternately from opposite ends along the fold edge. In diagrams E, F, and G, a square, a rectangle, and a circle are shown, folded several times and cut on alternate lines from opposite edges.

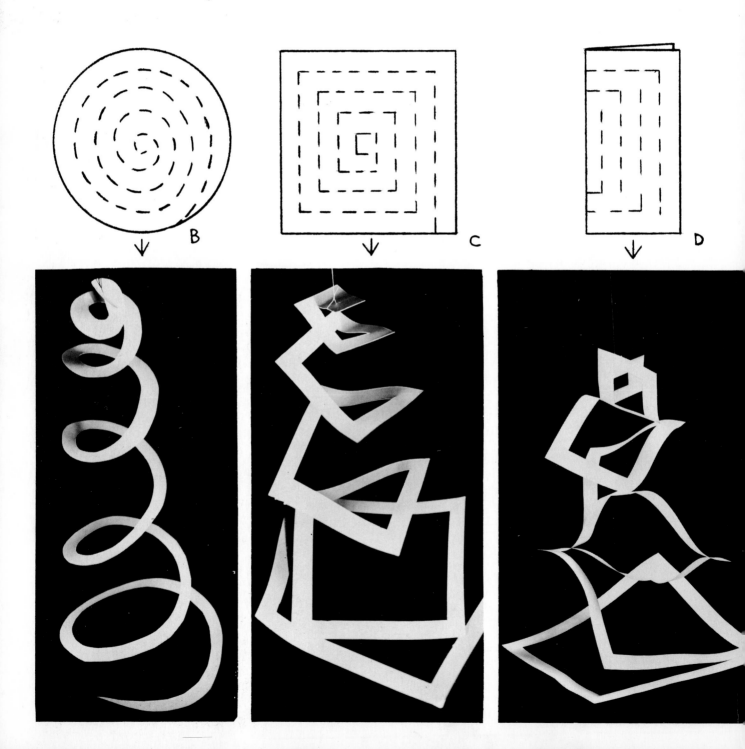

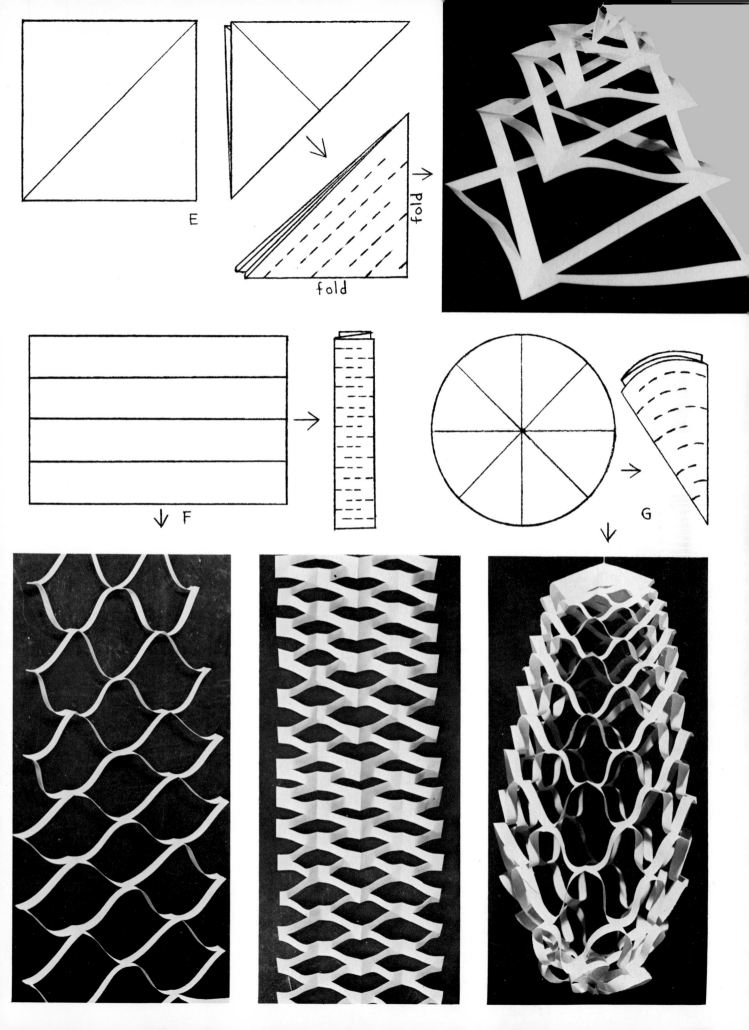

E

fold

fold

F

G

1

2

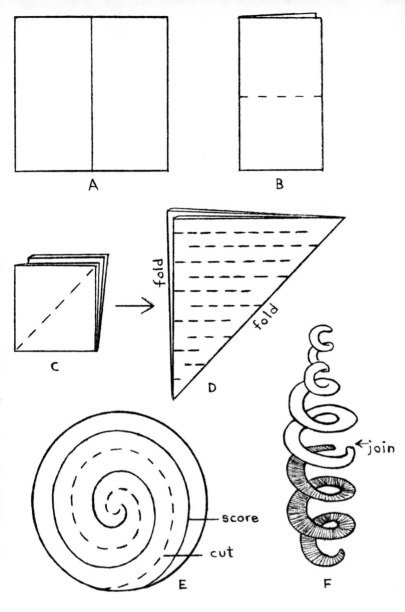

A

B

C

D

fold

fold

E

score

cut

F

join

Fascinating moving forms can be made from expanded structures like those on the facing page (diagrams E and F, above). The circle in figure 1 is cut and scored down the center of the strip (for scoring, see pages 46-48). The structure in figure 2 is formed of two spiral-cut circles, joined at their widest ends (for cutting circles, see diagram B, page 16). Several circles or squares can be joined to produce the structure at the right; for variety, use different sizes and colors. A plan for cutting the square is shown in diagrams A through D, above; for the circle, see diagram G, page 17. The centers can be removed to facilitate the joining of one part to another. Since forms made from thin papers stretch out longer, heavier paper is more suitable for use at the top to provide strength and rigidity. Colored Christmas balls or other items can be inserted within the structure.

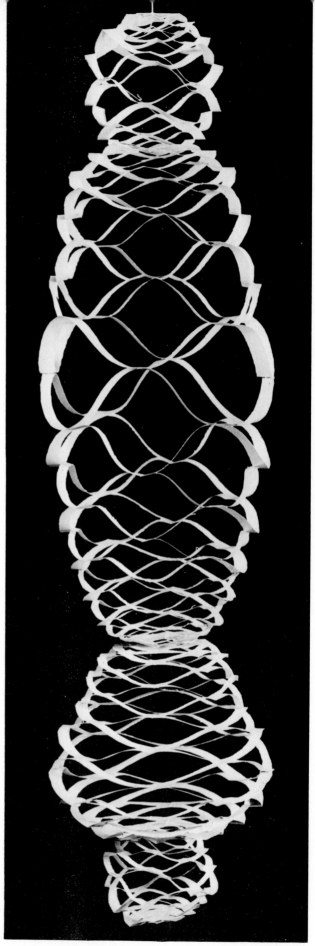

3

ONE-FOLD CUTTING

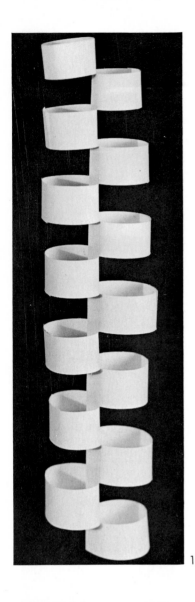

1

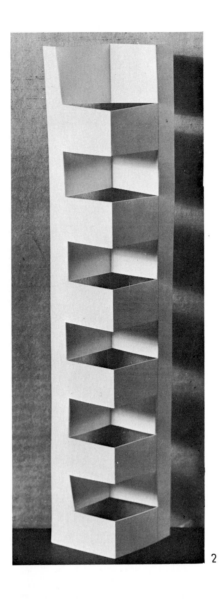

2

The structures shown here are all variations of one type of shape, where cuts are made either on the fold edge of the paper (diagram D) or on the outside edge (diagram F). The controlled lighting in the photographs helps to emphasize the relationship of planes where dark and light edges meet, so that abstract qualities are pronounced. Examples in the illustrations are used as suggestions showing some of the results made possible by this approach.

The interlocking structure in figure 4 (diagrams A, B, and C) is made by folding the paper in half in the center and creasing it in half again along line *cd*. The shape is refolded so that the two bottom edges are inside (diagram B). Slits are cut along the lower fold edges to within a half inch or so of the top fold, so that when opened up the structure appears as in diagram C. Alternate strips are bent forward and backward, with those in the left-hand section the reverse of those in the right-hand section. The two sections are then dovetailed.

The example in figure 5 is made by folding a rectangle in half twice and cutting slits part way inward on the folds of the opposite edges.

3

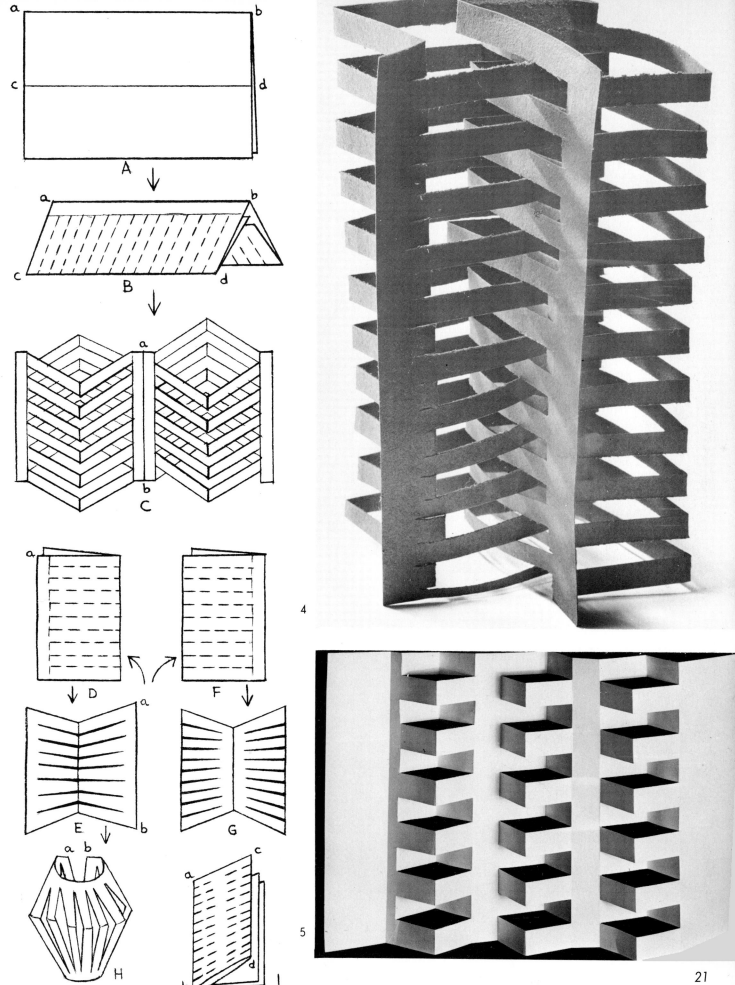

A

B

C

D

E

F

G

H

I

4

5

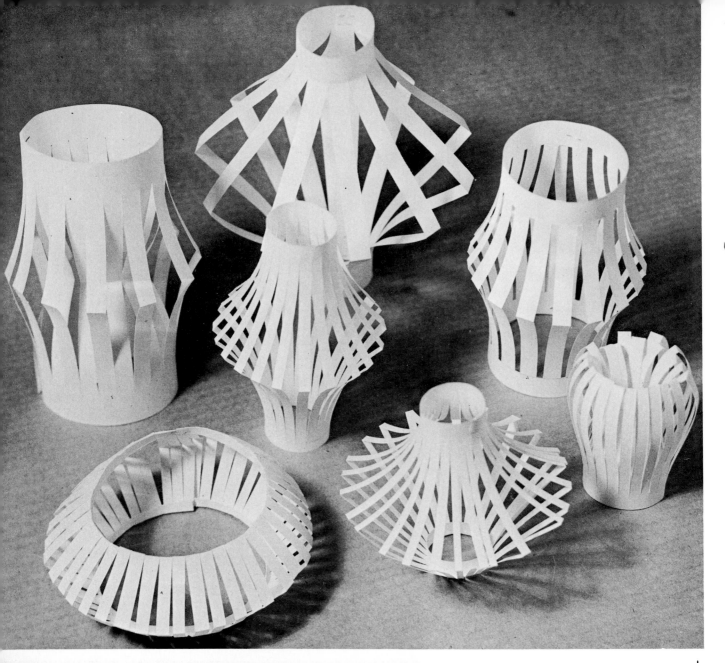

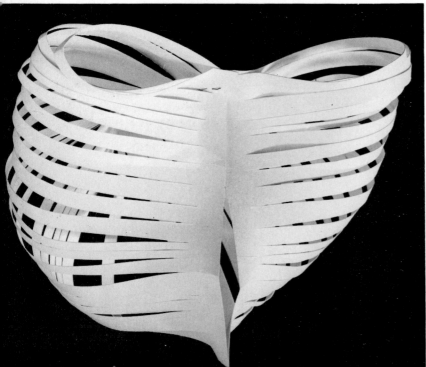

All of the structures on this page and the next are made from the same plan. Explanations for cutting and shaping the paper into a cylindrical form, held together with staples or cellophane tape, are given in diagrams B and C. Different forms can be achieved by variations in the sizes of the cuts, the weights and types of papers, and the relative proportions used. A multiple structure is produced by fastening several forms together and suspending them from above (diagram E). The use of Christmas tree balls or other ornaments in the enclosure adds a decorative quality.

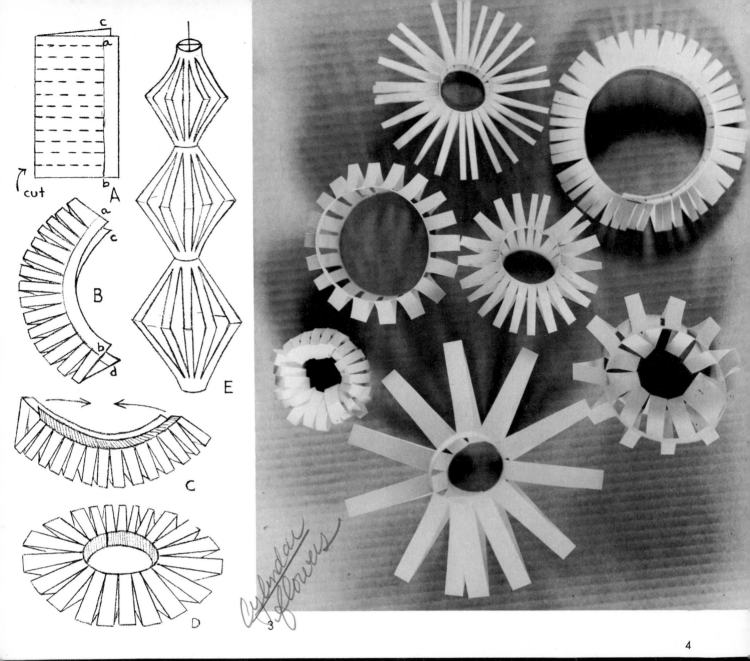

cut

A

B

C

D

E

Cylinder
flowers

3

4

SYMMETRICAL CUTTING

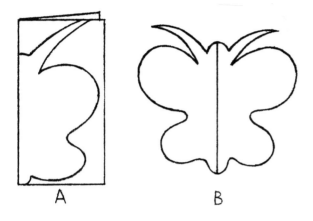

1

Some structures are pure in form, like those shown on the previous pages, while others are impressions derived from nature, like the butterfly shape used here for a subject source. The symmetrical cut is explained by the diagrams, and suggested variations with emphasis on a pleasing contour shape are shown in the photographs. In figure 1, several of the shapes are suspended on threads to hang like a mobile. The cutout of figure 2 is defined by placement over a contrasting color. Three symmetrical shapes, stapled together in the center and spread open, result in the form shown in figure 3, with bits of colored papers used for added interest.

2

3

MULTIPLE-FOLD CUTTING

1

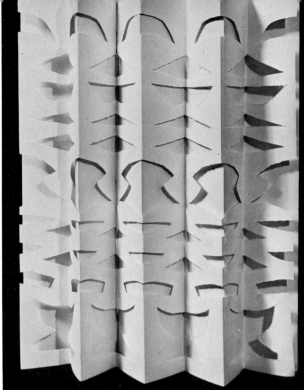

2

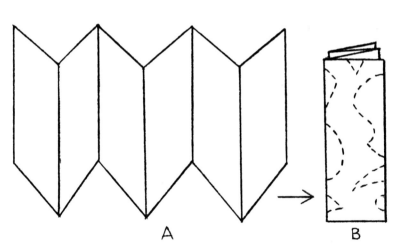

A   B

For the multiple-fold cut, the paper is folded a number of times and cut, with enough of the fold retained to enforce the structure. Rhythmic patterns of a traditional subject, cut by a child, are shown in figure 1. The cutout sections in the folded rectangle of figure 2 reveal the color of the folded paper underneath. The example in figure 3, of lightweight paper, has perforations made with a punch in the folded paper.

3

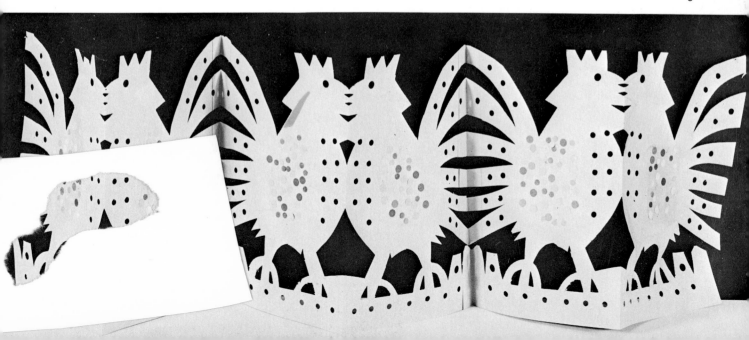

1

CUTOUTS

The folded paper technique, which always produces symmetrical shapes, is shown in squares, rectangles, and circles that have been folded alternately lengthwise and across for cutting. The resulting cutout openings make for dramatic contrasts of values, with larger and smaller intervals occurring in the rhythmic pattern. Interest is produced through varying the contours and sizes of the shapes. The dark areas made by cutting away the paper and the light ones that remain are equal in interest and balance and complement each other, creating positive-negative shape relationships. An example is shown in figure 2, where the positive shapes have been removed from the center of the cut and the negative shapes retained as part of the structure of the design. Some of the cutouts shown are traditional snowflake forms, which gain strength through their repetitive cuts.

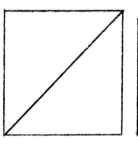
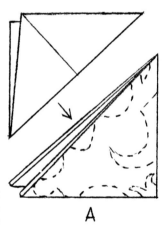

Fold square in half from corner to corner, then in half again. Cut shapes out of each side.

A

2

3

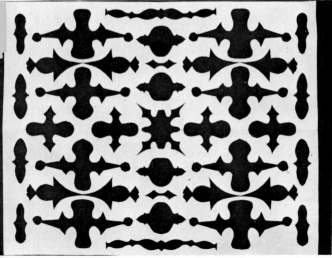
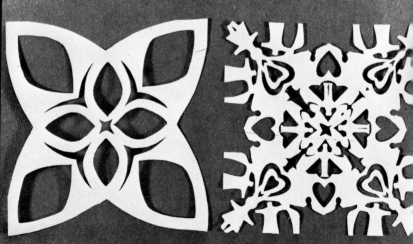

4

5

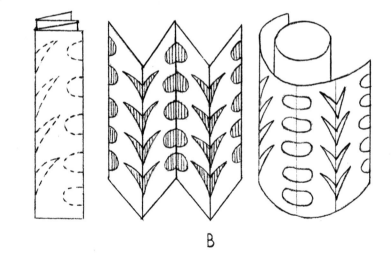

B

6

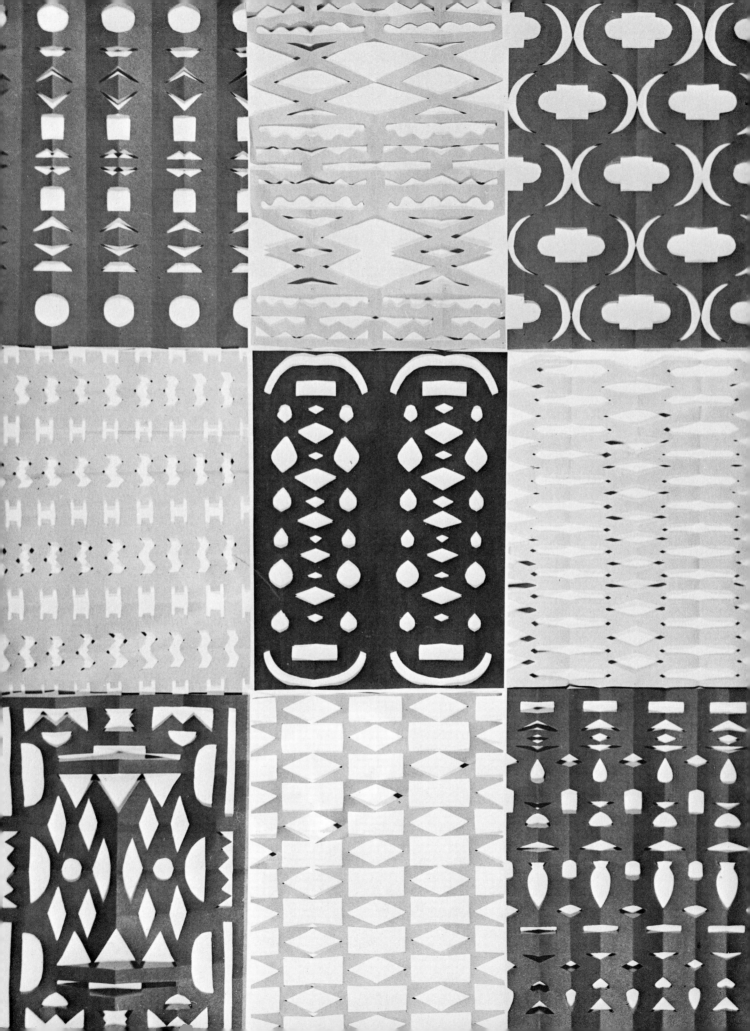

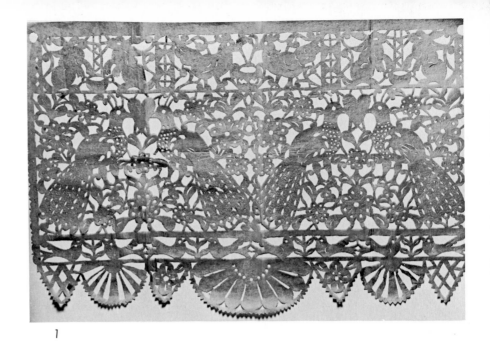

1

2

The paper cuttings on this page are representative of the folk art of many countries. Figures 1 and 2 are Mexican festival decorations cut from thin colored tissue papers. The Japanese stencil of rather tough paper in figure 3 is used for producing prints, but it has qualities making it beautiful as paper art regardless of the purpose it serves. The cutouts on the facing page are made from lightweight colored papers folded according to the directions in diagram B on page 27.

3

WINDOW CUTOUTS

1

2

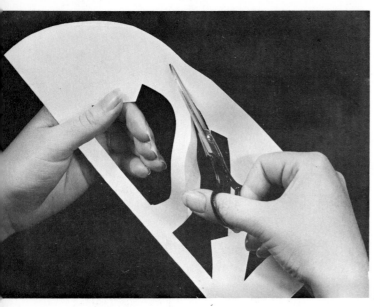

3

Symmetrical window cutouts are made from a folded sheet of paper with a rounded arc cut at the top. Inserts are removed with small, sharp scissors (figure 3). A solid border and part of the center fold should be retained. Figures 1 and 2 emphasize the line pattern; figures 3 and 4 (page 32) employ more solid area. The mantel decoration (page 31) is cut with a sharp knife from black paper and mounted on cardboard, with colored metallic papers inserted into the openings. In the richly imaginative composition on page 33, each area is removed with a sharp blade from an unfolded sheet of white construction paper, resulting in a rhythmical structural design.

1

2

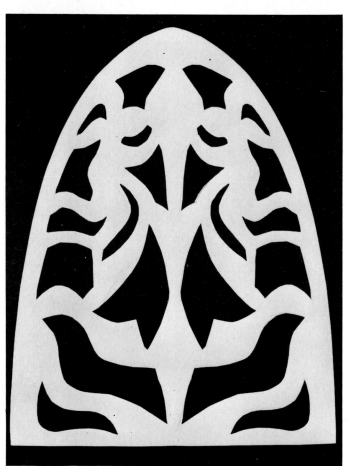

3

4

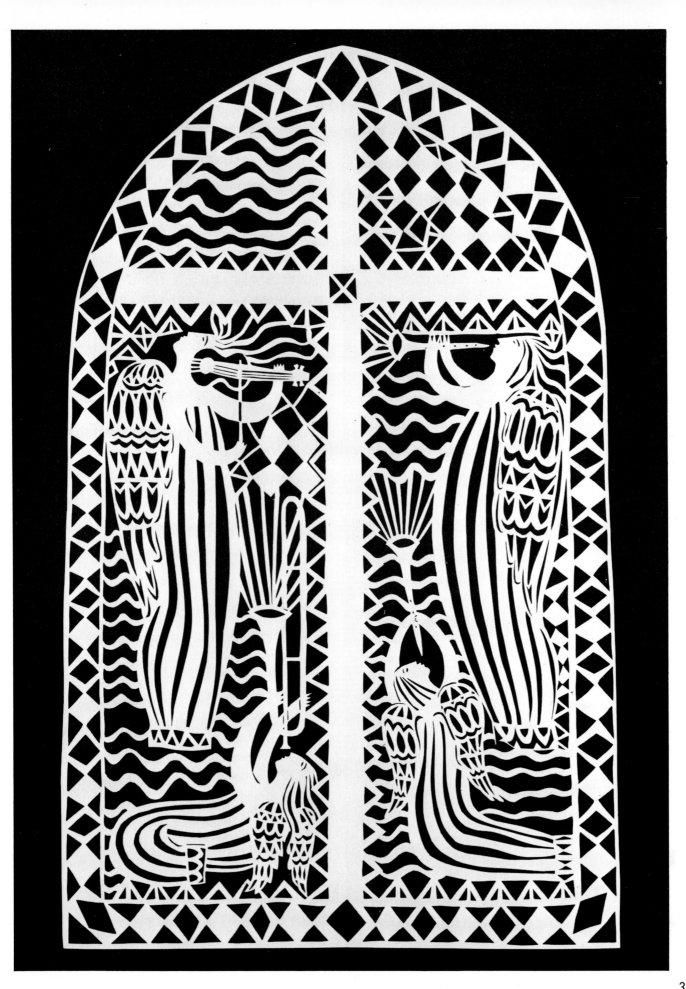

SURFACE TREATMENT

A textured pattern adds interest to paper by changing its surface appearance. For example, when paper is crushed in the hands, creases are produced which break up the surface structure so that it appears different in character. When slits are cut in the folded edges of the paper, opened, and bent outward, a three-dimensional effect is achieved (figure 1). Examples of cuttings made with both curved and straight edges are shown in figure 2, illustrating possibilities for such experiments. An application of this principle can be seen in the tree structure on the next page, where sections cut in the surface add a different textural effect. Figures 4 and 5 are compositions made by children, organizing flat and three-dimensional paper pieces to create surface variations. A paper punch was used for figure 6. An awareness of textured areas in nature as found in the rough-patterned bark of a tree or the overlapping bony shell of an armadillo will serve as source and inspiration for creating in paper.

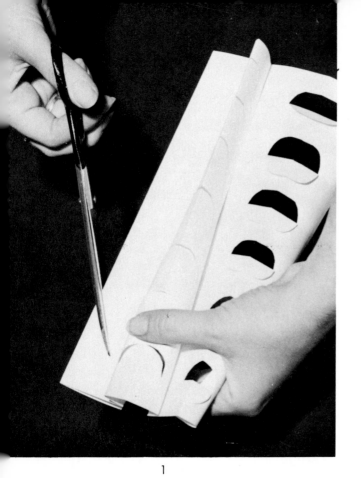

1

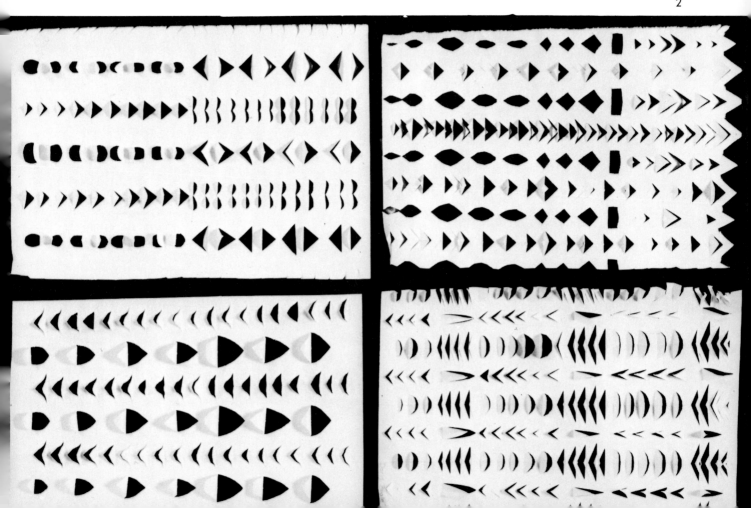

2

3

4

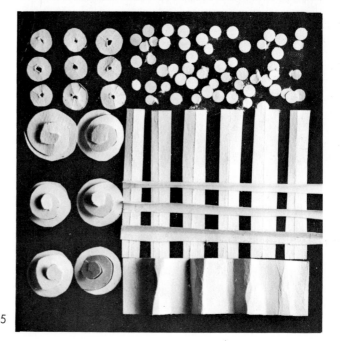

5

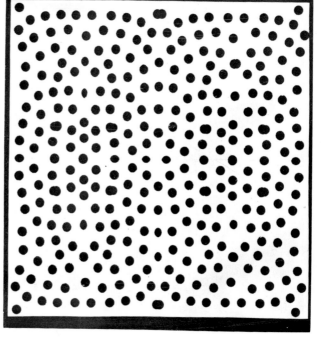

6

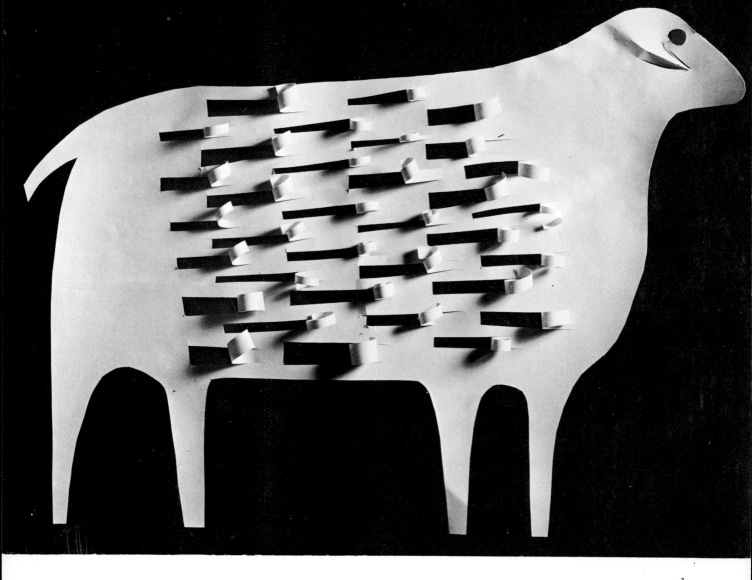

1

For the contoured lamb above, the flat surface is broken up with a patterned area produced by curling strips cut with a sharp blade and left attached on one side. The negative cut-out area balances with the positive shape of the strip, producing a dark-light contrast. The slit-scored ear and the perforated eye are part of the design qualities of the structure.

The rooster in figure 2 has a pleasing pattern on its surface as a result of the triangular shapes that have been slit on the sides and bent outward. The scored lines in the beak, comb, and tail are all part of the three-dimensional effect. (Scoring is explained on pages 46 and 47.) For the fish in figure 3, the paper was folded in half so that the two sides could be cut identically. Then slits were cut along the top fold, and folds were creased for cutting the side slits as shown in figure 1 on page 34. These examples are made of butcher paper and show how effective the use of a texture pattern can be in relieving a monotonous surface.

2

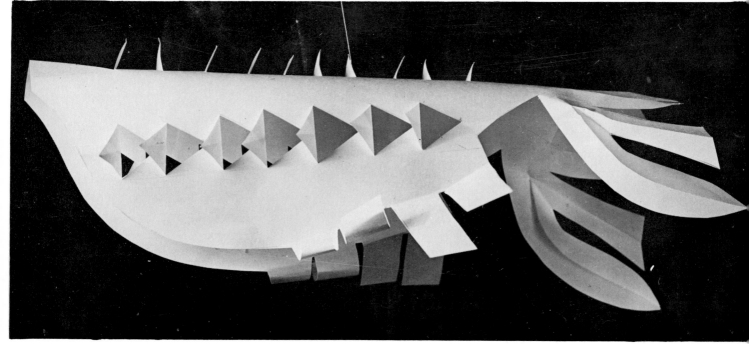

3

CURLING

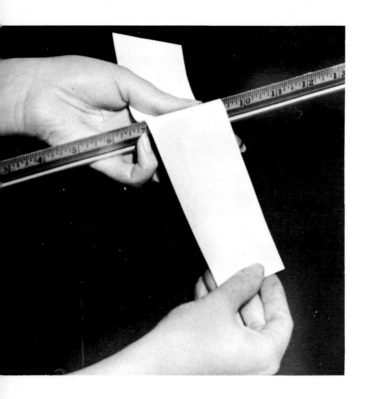

Pull paper tightly over ruler edge.

Roll paper around pencil to curl.

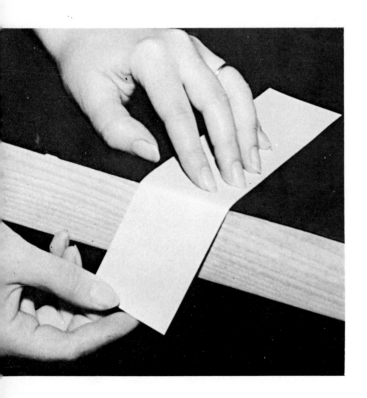

Pull paper over edge of table.

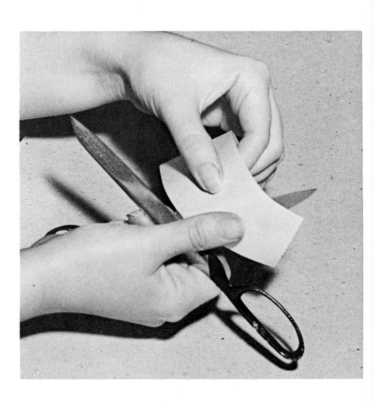

Stretch paper with scissors blade.

A

B

C

Curling adds interest and gives paper a three-dimensional quality. All papers, except the lightest in weight, can be curled more easily in one direction than another. By rolling paper in the hands it is possible to determine which direction is the most satisfactory. In some the grain is obvious, as in wood. Four ways to curl paper, using a ruler, pencil, table edge, and scissors, are shown on the facing page. A strip wrapped around the index finger will produce a loose curl, while one wrapped in a spiral around a pencil can be made into a diagonal curl. "Stripping" will make paper pliable so that it will roll easily. This can be done by placing the metal edge of a ruler on the paper, holding with a firm grip, and pulling the paper out from under. The paper is turned over and the process is repeated, the paper being stretched several times, first on one side and then on the other, until it rolls easily. The photograph below shows a fish construction with curled parts. For the lamb on page 112 and the Santa Claus on page 124, several strips are cut in one piece of paper and curled as shown in diagram B.

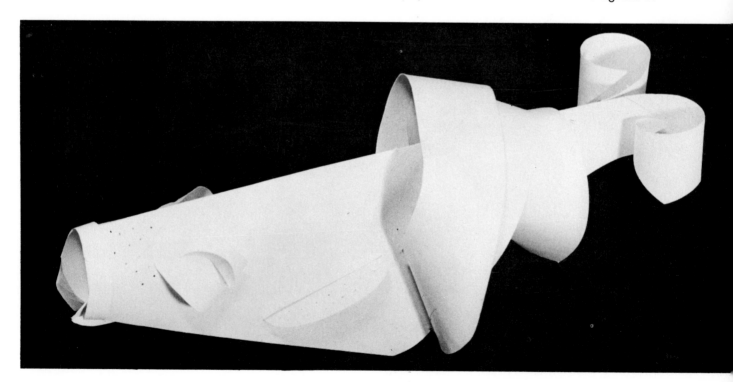

BENDING

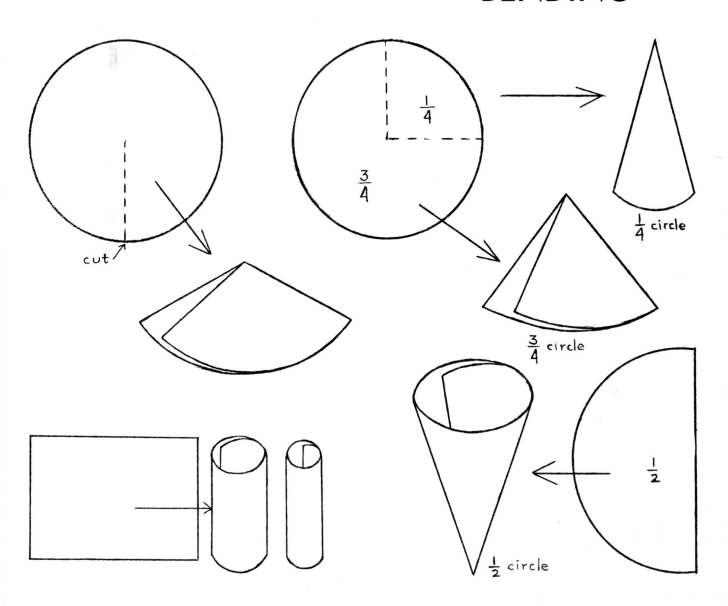

cut

$\frac{1}{4}$

$\frac{3}{4}$

$\frac{1}{4}$ circle

$\frac{3}{4}$ circle

$\frac{1}{2}$

$\frac{1}{2}$ circle

In the examples on the previous pages we have seen how paper can be modified by cutting and changed in surface character through various textural treatments. We now consider the three-dimensional form qualities of cones and cylinders produced by rolling or bending a sheet of paper into a volume. The cone is shaped from a circle or its parts, varying in proportions according to whether it is cut from a full circle, three-quarter circle, half circle, or quarter circle. The cylinder shape is produced by rounding a rectangle to the desired diameter. Cones and cylinders are used in a well-designed and integrated relationship in the creation of the bird structure, on the opposite page. Human figures, animals, fish, and angels are other subject sources shown in this book in which such forms have been used.

FOLDING

A

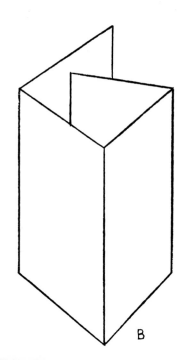

B

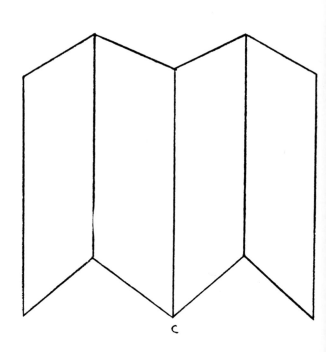

C

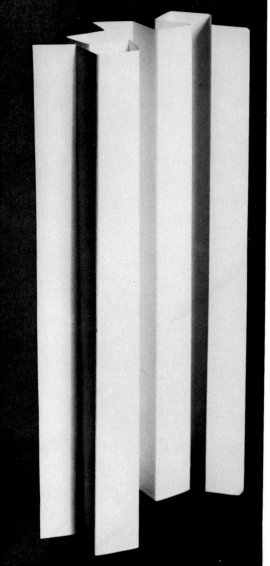

Folding translates paper into simple and exciting abstract three-dimensional formations that are basic to a great many constructions. Lightweight papers can be creased easily by hand without scoring. Papers with a pronounced grain fold more easily in one direction than in another. When folding paper it is helpful to crease it well with the thumbnail or the edge of a ruler. For accordion pleats, the paper is folded in half a number of times as in figure 1 on page 50. The result is a pleasing columnar structure (figure 1 at left) with creases that can be refolded back and forth to produce pleats like those in figure 3 or, spread out, as in diagram D. An application of this form is seen in the functional beauty of the fan. Folds like those in diagrams C and D are effective as backgrounds in showcases or with bulletin board arrangements.

1

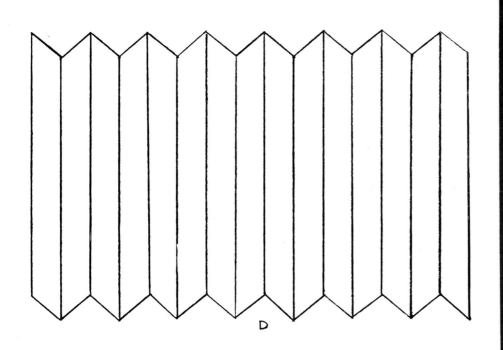

D

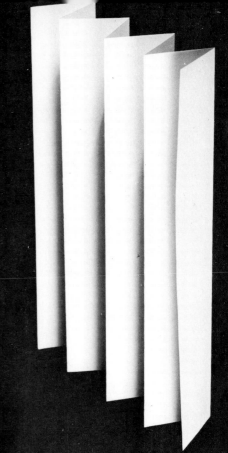

3

2

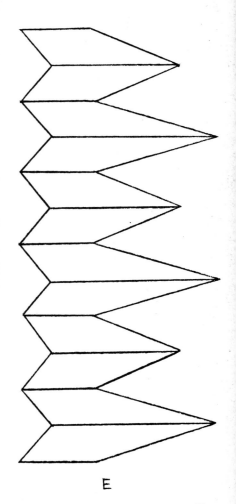

E

43

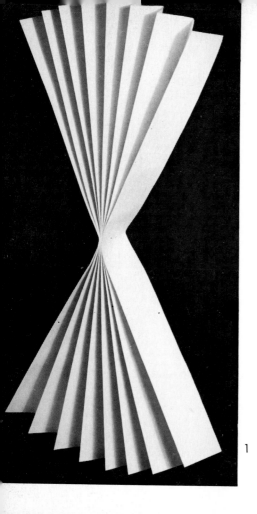

1

The structures here are a continuation of the approach presented on the previous page, with simple folded pleats appearing in different positions. Their beautiful abstract qualities are emphasized by the effects of light upon the sloping surfaces. The form on the facing page has strength as well as eye appeal and is capable of supporting considerable weight. It is rounded into a volume from a pleated rectangle, the edges being secured together with tape. A pleated piece of paper can inspire many experiments and should be explored for possible arrangements. Staples can be used to hold the form in the desired position. Shapes of this nature may suggest angel or bird wings. They can be used in combination with other forms as in the figure structures on pages 122 and 123.

fan fold flowers bend around + staple

2

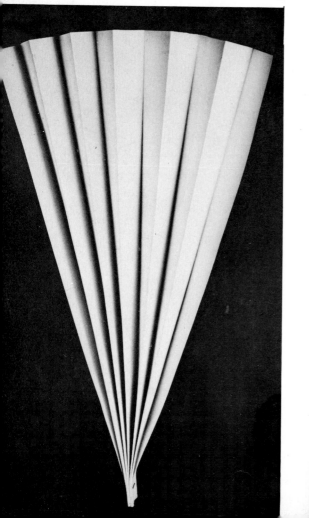

3

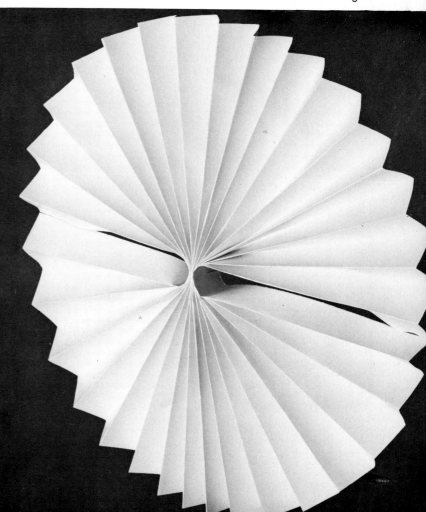

SCORING

Scoring is a process used in changing paper from a flat surface to one that is three-dimensional in structure. The results are the same as in folding or creasing, but with stiffer paper an instrument is needed to break down the fibers so that a neat edge will be secured and the paper will not crack when it is folded. The technique varies with the type of paper used. For construction paper a sharp, hard pencil will generally suffice, while for very heavy bond papers a dull knife is satisfactory. A smooth scissors blade, compass point, or nail file is also recommended for use. Parchment papers must be carefully scored to avoid ragged edges, and since they are translucent, pencil lines will show through. The best method can be determined by experimenting on scrap paper. If the paper is not very heavy, all scoring can be done on one side only and the folds bent in either direction. If it is rigid, like heavy Bristol or chipboard, every other line must be scored on the reverse side of the paper before folding.

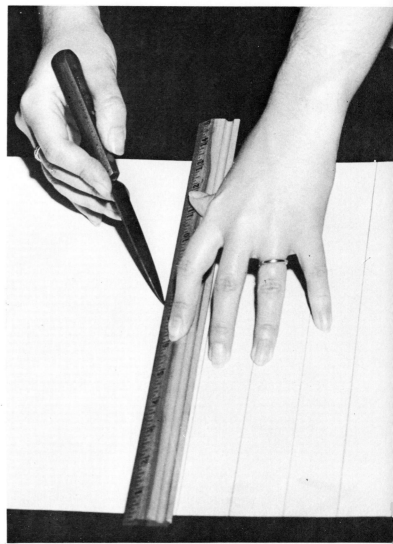

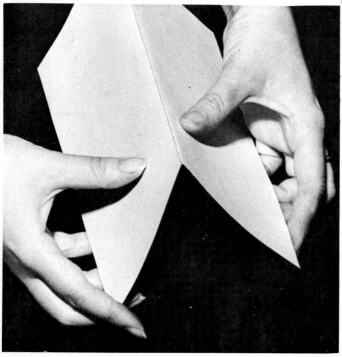

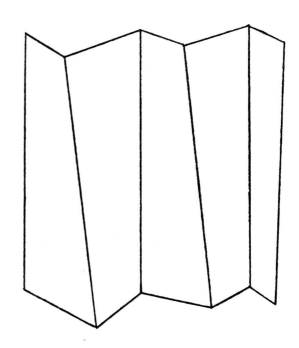

1

2

3

4

Curves are beautiful structures when scored. Shown are a number of different kinds that may be constructed freehand or with the use of a French curve. It is advisable to experiment with making a single curve at first, then reverse curves, and more complex ones later. Paper scored with a curved line no longer remains flat but becomes three-dimensional. When two lines are scored, one bends in the opposite direction from the other. Applications of scored curves will be found throughout the book.

A circle becomes a three-dimensional structure when it is slit to the center and scored. Any number of lines can be drawn on the circle with a compass and then scored. When the cut edges of the circle are overlapped, a cone is formed, as shown in these examples. In scored parts, a convex surface is always adjacent to a concave one. An application of the scored circle can be seen in the eye of the fish construction in figure 7. Figures 4, 5, and 6 show other variations.

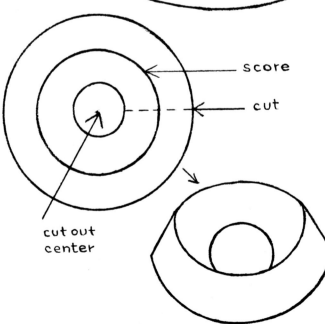

1

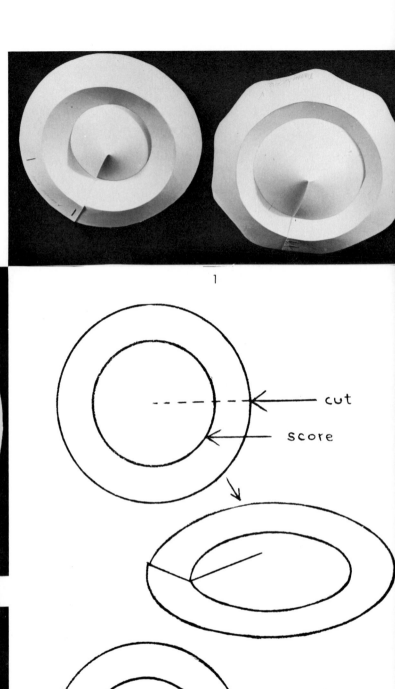

2

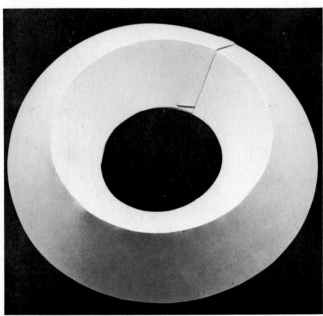

3

cut

score

score

cut

cut out center

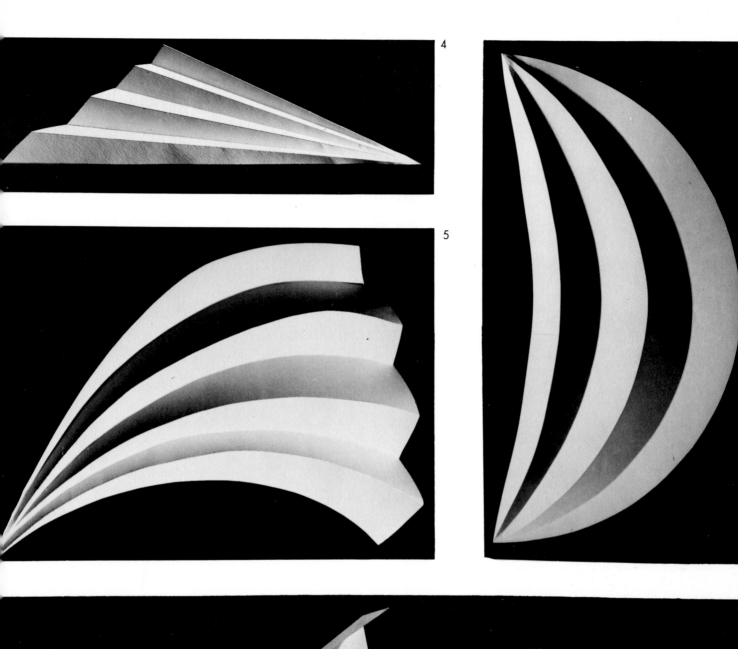

4

5

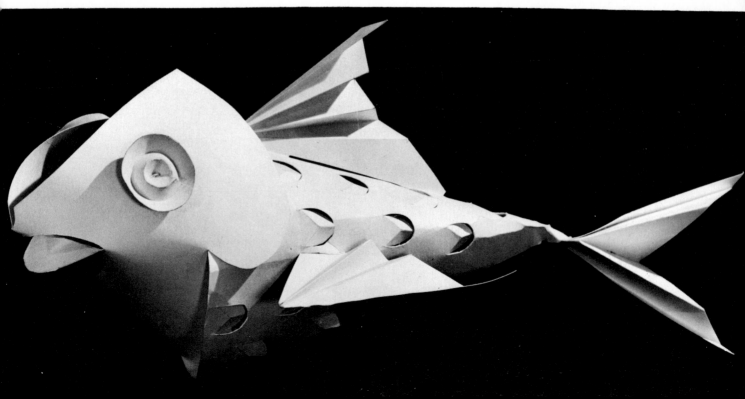

1

2

In order to understand the principle of scoring, it is helpful to refer again to folding. The beginner can grasp the meaning of transforming a flat piece of paper into a three-dimensional structure by folding a lightweight sheet like bond or construction paper in half as shown in figure 1. After it has been folded several times until the desired width is achieved, it will look like figure 1 on page 42. Folding the creases backward and forward so that every other crease is up, and the alternate ones are down, results in an accordion-pleated effect. Scoring is built upon a structure like this, with more complicated arrangements and planes moving in various directions, as will be noted in subsequent pages.

Curves, unlike straight lines, cannot be creased without first being scored with an instrument like a dull knife or scissors. They permit the direction of a line to be changed, and can be drawn free-hand or with the use of a French curve on a flat piece of paper. After scoring, every other line is bent upward and alternate lines go down to produce a three-dimensional effect. See figures 3, 4, and 5.

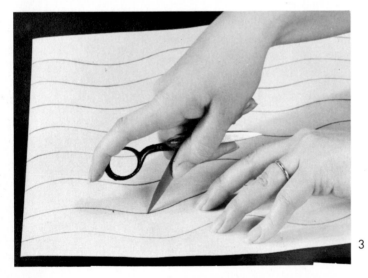

3

5

4

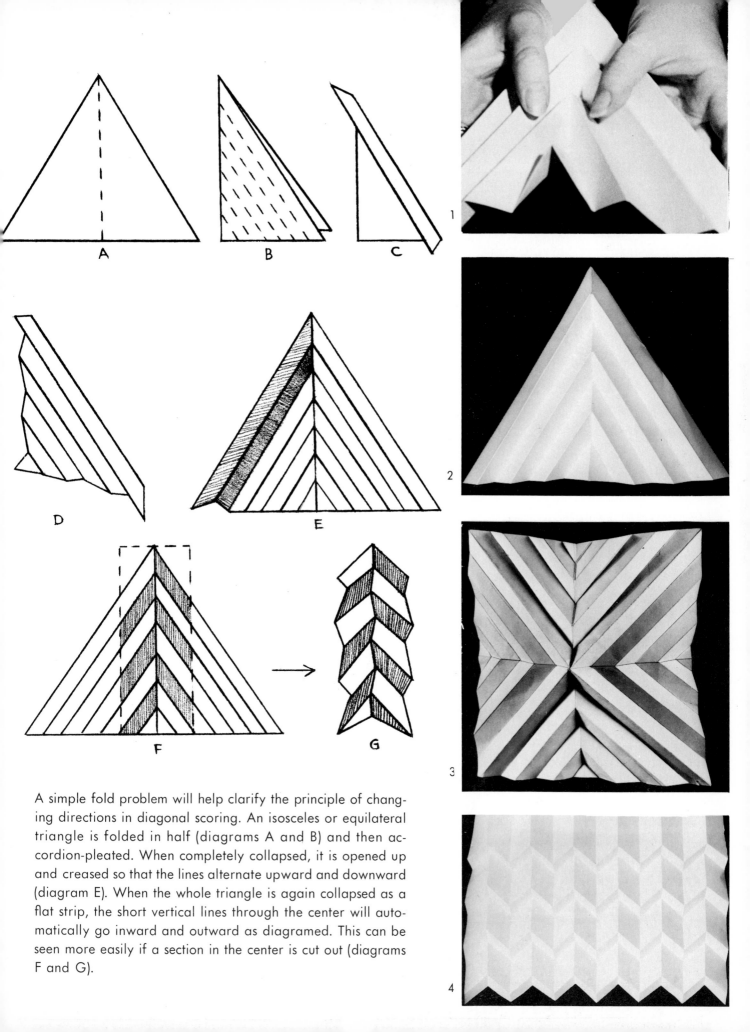

A B C

D E

F → G

1

2

3

4

A simple fold problem will help clarify the principle of changing directions in diagonal scoring. An isosceles or equilateral triangle is folded in half (diagrams A and B) and then accordion-pleated. When completely collapsed, it is opened up and creased so that the lines alternate upward and downward (diagram E). When the whole triangle is again collapsed as a flat strip, the short vertical lines through the center will automatically go inward and outward as diagramed. This can be seen more easily if a section in the center is cut out (diagrams F and G).

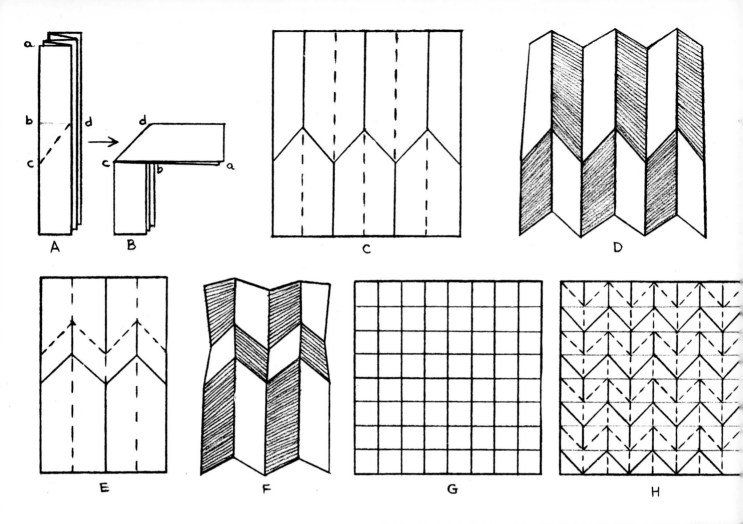

A   B   C   D

E   F   G   H

The principle of diagonal scoring, illustrated in the beautiful Finnish paper at the right, is explained by simple folding techniques with lightweight paper in the diagrams on this page. An understanding of this process can lead to many exciting variations of the same scoring principle. A sheet of paper folded in half several times is again folded (diagram B) at the mid-mark to form a right angle, then opened flat. The diagonal folds are creased in the same direction while the verticals alternate upward and downward (diagrams C and D). The paper will begin to round into a volume as shown in figure 2 on page 63. If several rows of diagonals are folded at equal distances apart, the paper will remain parallel to the table. A grid can be constructed with pencil and diagonals drawn upon it and scored with a pointed instrument. Dotted lines indicate downward creases.

A paper study from the Arts and Crafts and Industrial Design School of Helsinki, Finland (product design class; Ilmari Tapiovaara, adviser).

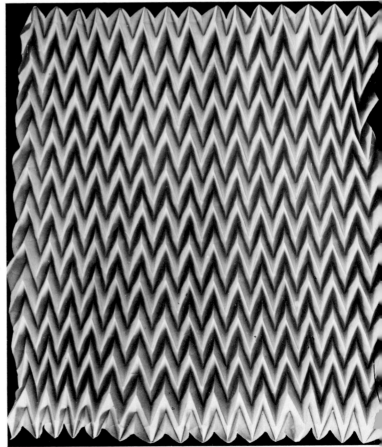

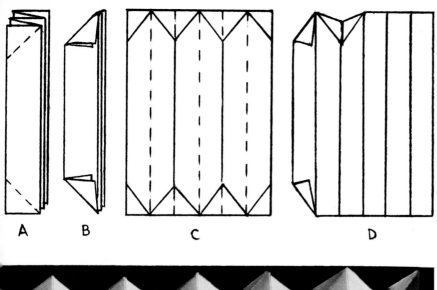

A   B   C   D

The diagrams on this page continue explanations of the principles of scoring by means of simple folding plans. An accordion-pleated strip (diagram A) with the top and bottom ends folded (diagram B) provides the basic creases, which can be maneuvered into a form like that shown in figure 1. The paper must be opened and the folds reshaped to take alternate directions—the solid lines one way, the dotted lines another. At first manipulating the paper in this way will seem awkward, but facility in handling such folds comes with practice. It is very helpful to collapse the paper by flattening the creases while folding them. Figure 2 shows how one hand can support the structure and crease it from underneath while the fingers of the other straddle the pleats on top.

1

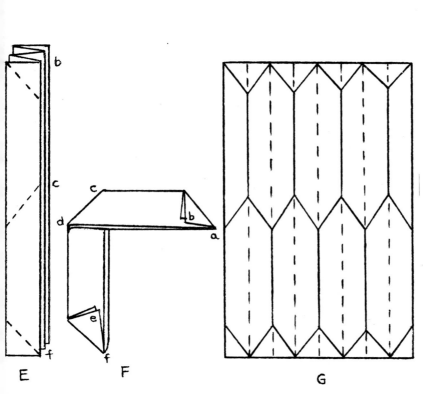

E   F   G

2

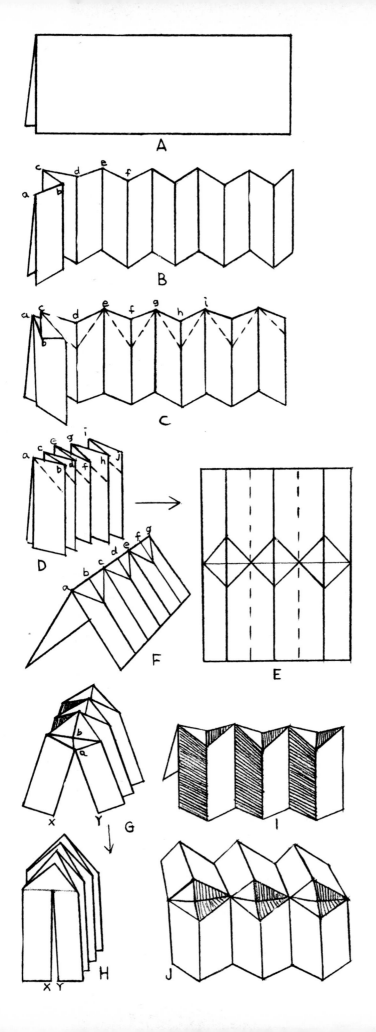

These diagrams show another approach to scoring demonstrated by the folding technique. A lightweight sheet of paper is folded in half and then into pleats. The top of each pleat is creased downward at right angles, bent backward, and creased again, as in diagrams B, C, and D. When the paper is opened up flat it reveals diamond shapes creased in the center. The long verticals are then refolded into accordion pleats, and the structure is spread out like a tent (diagram F). Looking down on the diamond shapes, begin at the end marked x and y and push the horizontal crease downward at b (diagram G). Pull x and y together until they meet, forcing the diagonal creases of the diamond upward. Continue collapsing each diamond flat as in diagram H. When the paper is stretched out again (diagram I), the recessed diamonds appear. A top view (diagram J) shows the paper beginning to round into a volume. An application of this principle is shown in figure 3 on page 63. See also the directions on pages 52 and 53.

The beautiful cylindrical shape on the facing page is made from a sheet of butcher paper about 20 by 30 inches in size. It is based upon the grid plan of diagram H on page 56, constructed without drawing but entirely by folding and creasing. First the verticals are folded, with all the creases on the same side of the paper rather than alternating as with pleats. The paper is then turned over and the first diagonal line creased, starting at the upper left corner and counting over eight spaces at the bottom. This is continued until all the diagonal lines are creased in one direction. Then the lines going from the upper right to lower left are creased so that diamond shapes are created by the crossing of the diagonals. All lines must be sharply creased. Starting at one end, collapse the folds together, forming the shape shown in the photograph. This makes a structure approximately 14 inches high and 7½ inches in diameter. The outer edges are fastened together and a flat covering put on the top and bottom.

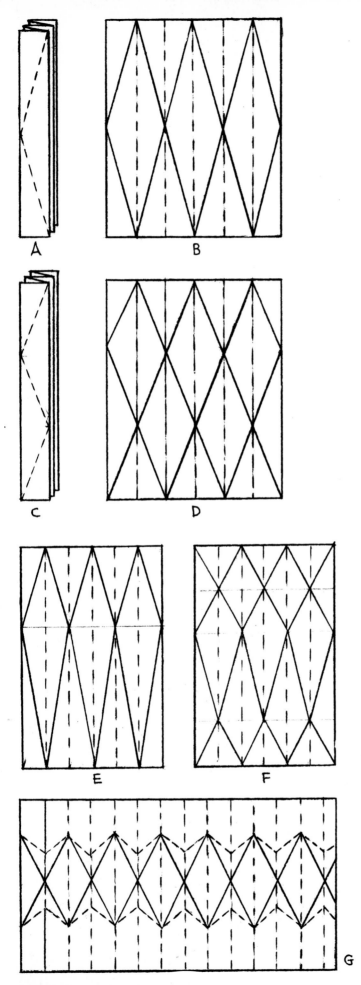

A convex structure can be formed of diagonal shapes rounded into a volume as explained in the diagrams here. The deeper the facets, the more sudden the rounding of the volume, while narrower facets provide for a more gradual form. The form of the volume is controlled by the number of the diagonal shapes as well as by their length, width, and contour. The application of this principle is shown on the previous pages, in figure 3 on page 65, and in the Easter eggs on page 158.

A lightweight sheet of paper is folded in half several times as in figure 1 on page 50. While the paper is still folded, it is creased on the dotted lines from the center of one edge to the opposite corners (diagram A). All the vertical lines are creased on one side of the paper; then the paper is turned over so that the diagonal lines can be creased on the other side. The diagonals can also be folded by creasing the paper from the top of one vertical over to the bottom of the paper two spaces over (diagram E). On heavier paper these lines have to be drawn with a pencil and scored with a pointed instrument.

For a more complicated arrangement, the paper can be folded and creased with three diagonal lines (diagram C). Any number of diamond shapes can be created by introducing more creased diagonals.

Suggested variations are shown in diagrams F and G. Other plans can also be tried. A volume can be constructed by folding the diagonals eight spaces over (diagram H), as shown in the cylinder form on page 55.

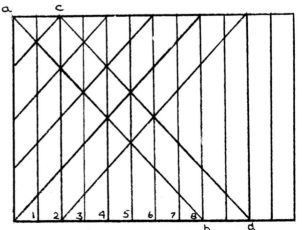

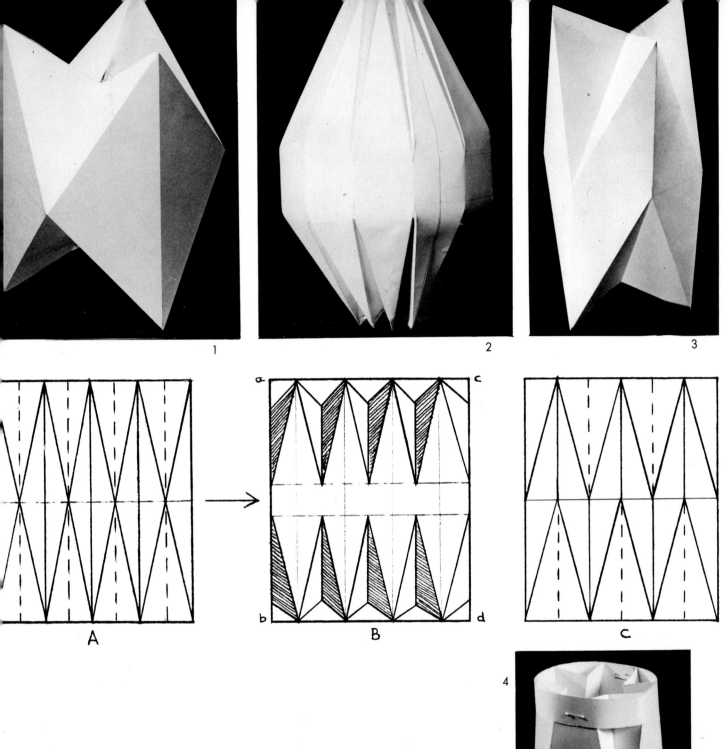

1

2

3

A

B

C

4

All of the volumes on this page are created from the same basic plan with slight variations and changes in proportion. In figure 1 the diamond shapes are broader across, while in figure 2 they are narrow and separated by a band through the center. In figure 3 the parallel diagonal lines are all creased on the same side of the paper so that they come forward, while the verticals are creased to recede. The outside edges are fastened together to hold the volume in position. The diagrams indicate the plans used in each of the photographs.

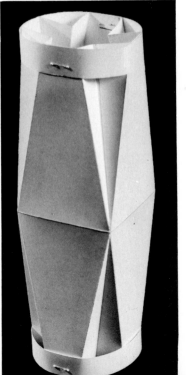

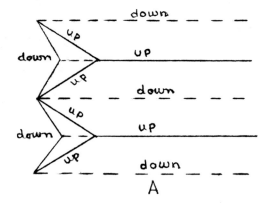

A

The scorings on the facing page are made according to the plan on page 53. The position of the scored creases in figure 1 is explained in diagram A, which shows how the lines alternate with one another. When one crease goes down or inward, the adjoining one comes upward. In making this scoring it is possible to work on either side of the paper by just turning it over. Figure 2 is an extension of the diagrams on page 53. Figure 3 is composed of two sheets of lightweight colored papers, scored or creased as in figure 1 and stapled together through the center while collapsed. It is then spread out and stapled together at the outer edges to form a circular shape.

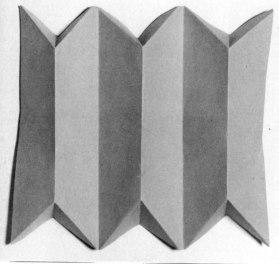

1

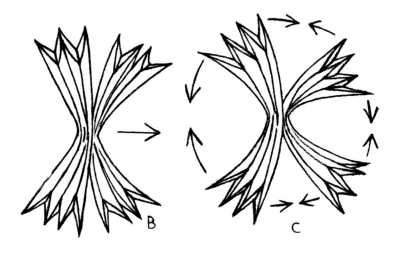

B   C

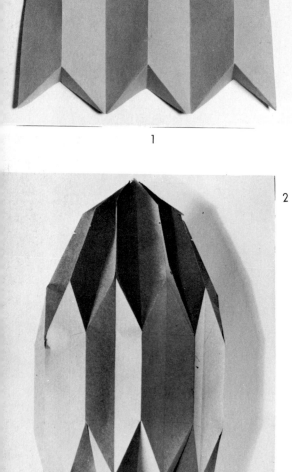

3

2

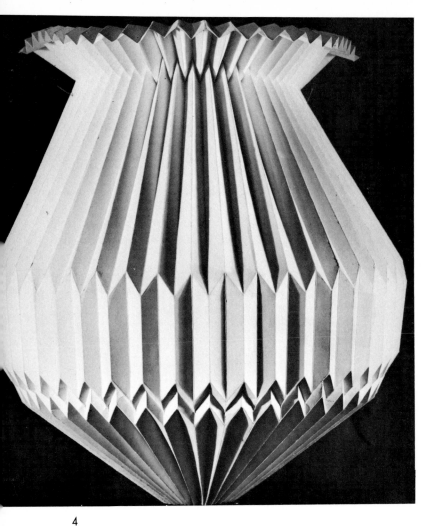

4

5

Different volumes are created by changing the length and width of facets as well as the proportional lengths of the diagonal lines, all controlling factors in the outcome of the shape. The examples shown here are based primarily on the approaches explained on pages 53 and 58, but include more detail at the top and bottom of the structure. When forms like these are used as light shades, the paper should be prevented from touching a hot light bulb or it will be scorched. An application of water glass is sometimes effective as a protective coat but should be tried out first on a scrap of paper. To give a translucent quality to the paper, a mixture of half shellac and half alcohol can be applied, or linseed oil can be used.

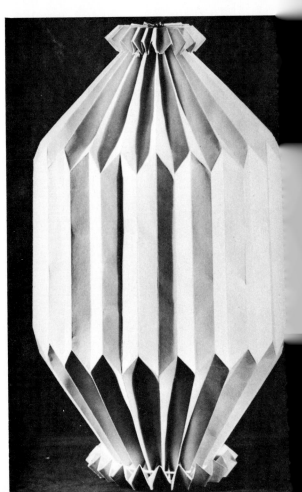

6

2

The volumes on this page, although different in shape, are based upon the same type of scoring. Figure 1, made of white construction paper, has the added interest of color applied with a brush and water paint. Figure 2 is made of medium-weight butcher paper, as is figure 3, page 65.

The form of the structure is controlled by the kind of pleats employed. Long pleats with long points will result in an elongated structure, while shorter pleats will permit the form to round out, with more paper being required for the fuller width. The following steps explain the procedures necessary to construct this type of volume.

First determine the size of the structure desired and the dimensions of the paper needed. For a structure like that in figure 2, a sheet about 14 by 50 inches will give a circumference of 28 inches.

Draw the required grid plan with a sharp pencil and ruler, using light lines (diagram A). Score the vertical lines the entire length of the paper, and then score the diagonal lines. The hori-

I

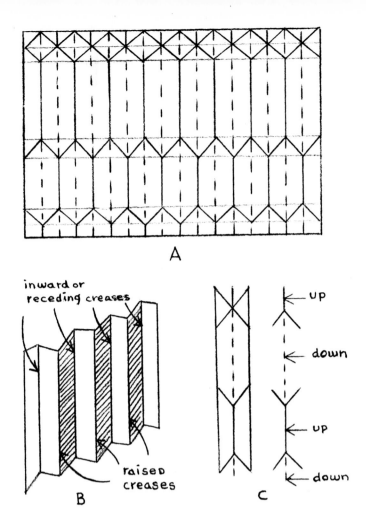

A

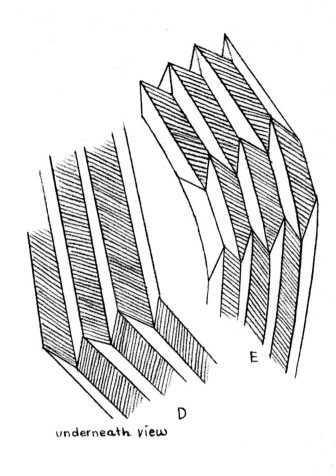

inward or receding creases

raised creases

B

up
down
up
down

C

D

underneath view

E

zontal lines are not scored. Bend the vertical lines into an accordion fold (diagram B). The vertical lines must be recreased so that they are up where the solid lines are indicated in diagram A, and down where the dotted lines are shown. See diagram C for a more detailed explanation. To accomplish this, place the fingers of one hand between the folds and, holding the folds in place, raise the diagonals and fold the verticals in or out. At first this may seem awkward, but do not be discouraged. Each person works out his own system for achieving results after he once understands the principles involved. In order to become familiar with the procedure, it is well to practice first on something like typing paper, which is easily creased.

The alternation of creases upward and downward changes a flat sheet of paper into a volume, as shown in diagrams D and E.

Pull the top and bottom together as in figure 3, and secure with thread or a rubber band. Fasten the edges together with rubber cement or staples.

3

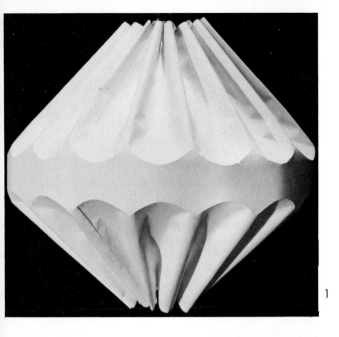

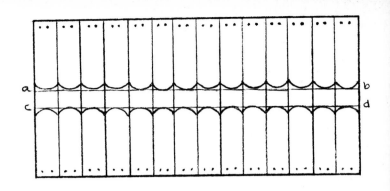

Start with a rectangle and draw lines ab and cd on either side of the center. Divide into vertical spaces. Draw curves and score each one. Punch holes at top and bottom and gather with thread. Do not crease or score the vertical lines. The scored curves can be varied by changing the size and proportions.

1

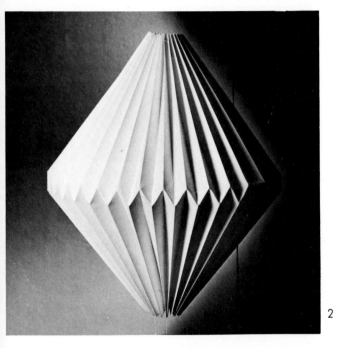

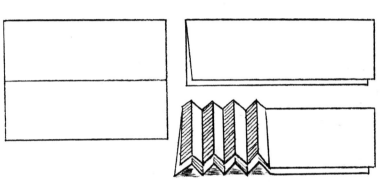

Fold a rectangle in half through the center. Fold into even pleats. Open the paper and staple the edges together to form a cylinder. Gather top and bottom by running a needle and thread through the folds.

2

3

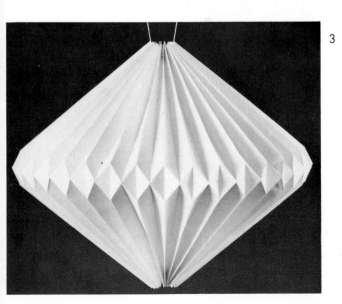

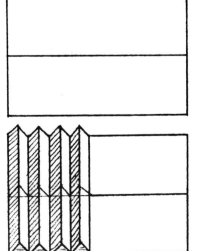

To make figure 3 see directions on page 54. For the bottom light shade on the facing page crease a rectangle through the center and open it up. Fold or score the pleats. Punch holes at top and bottom and gather with thread.

The cone-shaped structure in figure 2, constructed of white engineering detail paper from a sheet 2 yards in length and 14 inches in width, results in a form approximately 60 inches in circumference. The plan used for scoring is shown in diagrams A and B; the horizontal lines are guides only and are not scored. If paper is scored too heavily, it will break through. After scoring, the paper is turned over and creased on the opposite side to avoid having the pencil lines show. It is usually easier to crease the verticals first and then the diagonals. Holes are punched near the top, and a thread is run through to pull the pleats together.

Figure 4 is a detail section of a scored light shade with the lower edge folded up. The plan is shown in diagram D. To avoid having pencil lines show, the paper can be creased directly, but the bottom part of the diagram must be drawn on the reverse side to coordinate the folding. All vertical and diagonal lines are scored, and the vertical pleats are creased the full length of the paper as in diagram E. The scoring in the top section of diagram D is shown in detail in diagram F; the bottom section is creased more conveniently by turning the paper over (diagram G). The bottom section can be folded up an inch or more on line ab (diagram H) so that the creases fall in and fit with the vertical pleats shown in diagram I, or it can be left down. The paper is pulled together at the top.

Figure 1 shows a structure made of a sheet of paper folded double with the fold edge on the bottom. Another plan is shown in diagram C.

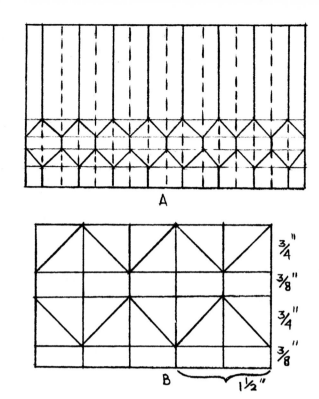

A

B

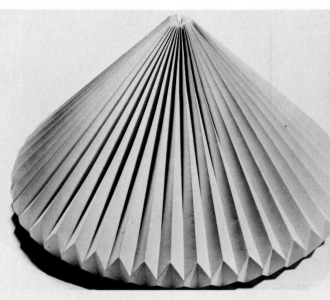

2

1

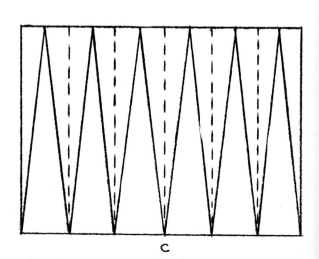

C

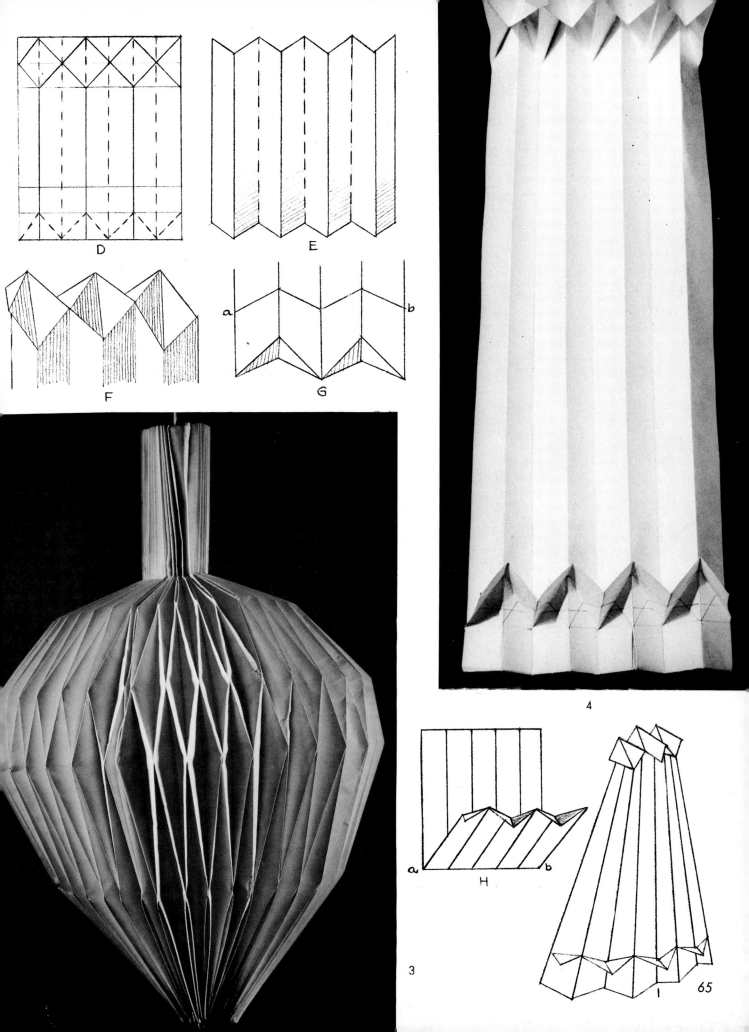

D

E

F

G

a   b

4

H

a   b

3

65

I

VARIATIONS WITH CUTS

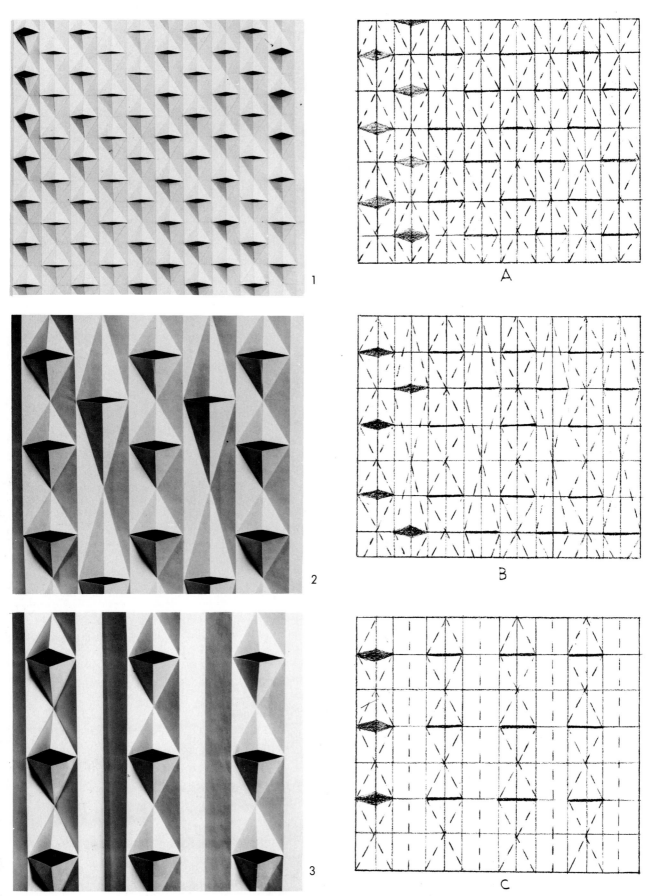

1

2

3

A

B

C

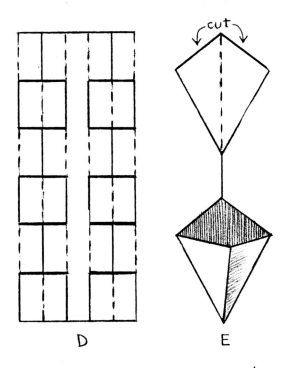

D

E

These abstract structures have an exciting quality resulting from combinations of scored lines and slit or pierced openings. The adjacent diagrams show the plans used. Slit sections are indicated by the heavy lines which, when cut and opened, appear as diamond shapes. Dotted lines are bent inward, and solid lines come forward; horizontal lines are used as guides only. The paper can be cut with a sharp knife, a razor blade, or a mat cutter. A piece of cardboard placed underneath absorbs the pressure and protects the table surface. Figure 5, explained in diagram E, has been rolled into a cylinder shape. The examples shown are suggestions that can be varied to suit the ideas of the designer. Such structures can be used effectively as backgrounds for displays and exhibits, or as inserts for screens as shown on pages 68 and 69. When rounded they can serve as light shades.

4 5

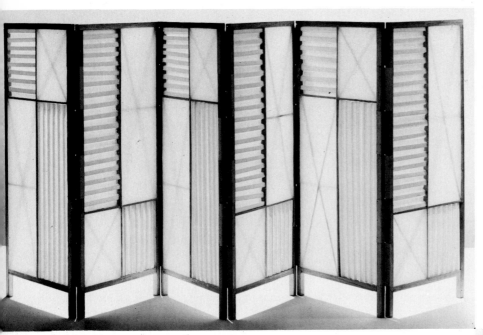

SCREEN

MODELS

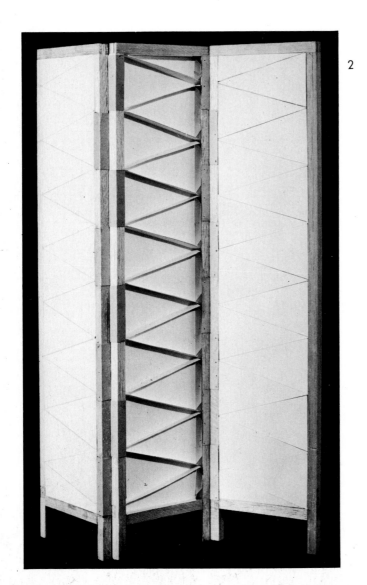

1

2

3

4

Paper screens are familiar items in Oriental interiors and in contemporary settings. These examples are small scale models of balsa wood frames with paper structure inserts, presented as suggestions with possibilities for development into full-size room dividers or backgrounds. In figure 1, plain areas of paper backed with wood strips are combined with scored sections. The examples in figures 2 and 3 are constructed of triangular shapes attached with bent tabs on each side.

In the photograph below, a screen model is used as background for paper furniture structures to show how various elements can be related to form a room composition. The screens shown here have hinges made of strips of a sturdy fabric (diagram A) which hold the two adjoining posts together and permit the sections to be turned either forward or back.

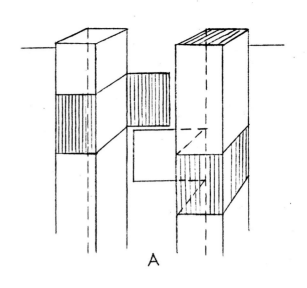

A

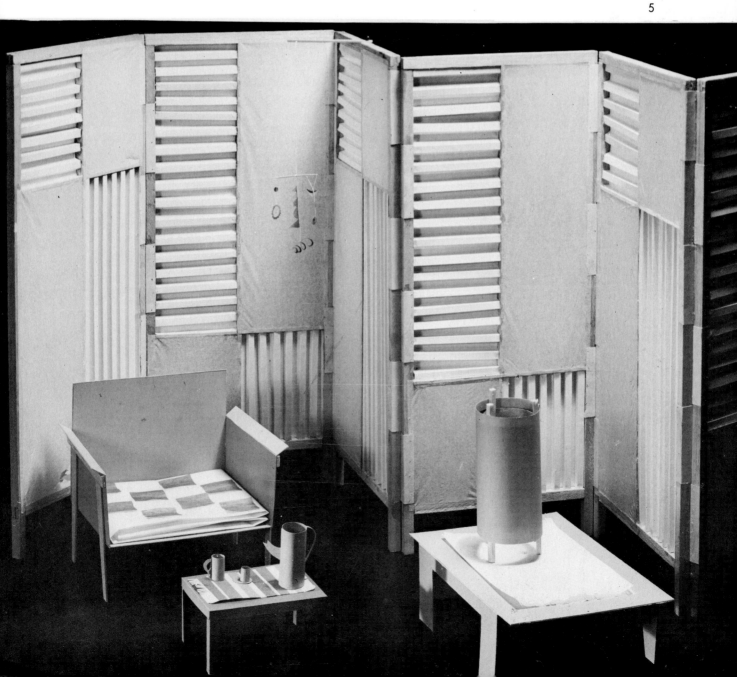

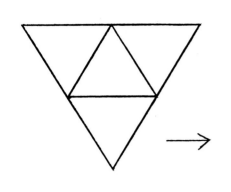

GEOMETRIC SOLIDS

1

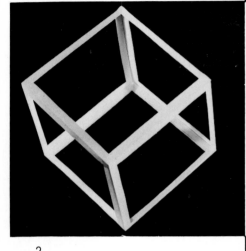

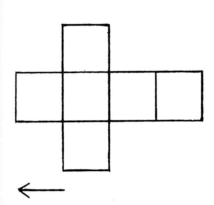

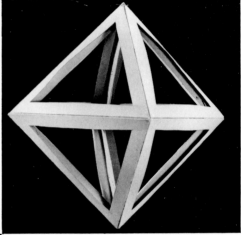

2

3

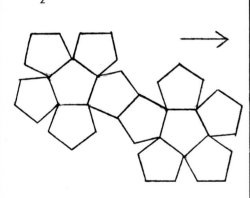

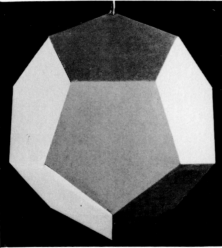

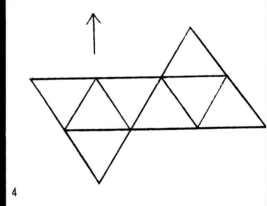

4

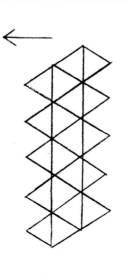

5

There are five regular geometric solids, including: (1) tetrahedron (four sides); (2) hexahedron or cube (six sides); (3) octahedron (eight sides); (4) dodecahedron (twelve sides); (5) icosahedron (twenty sides). Whether with open surfaces or closed, these volumes can be the basis for paper structure.

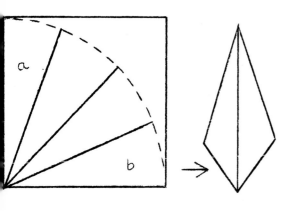

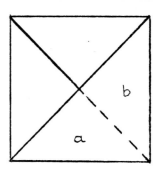

Draw an arc in a square to form a quarter circle. Divide into four or five equal parts. Cut on dotted line. Fold on lines and lap a over b. To vary proportions, use a half circle.

Cut dotted line. Lap a over b.

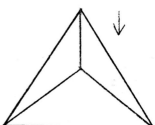

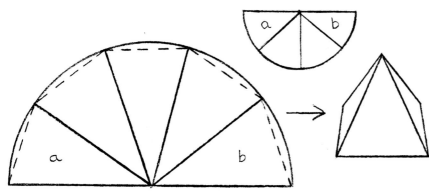

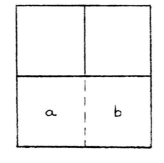

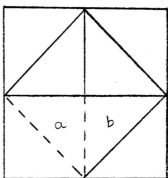

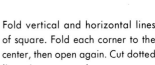

Fold vertical and horizontal lines of square. Fold each corner to the center, then open again. Cut dotted lines. Lap a over b.

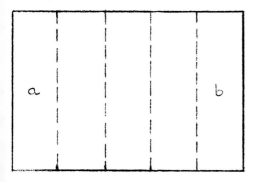

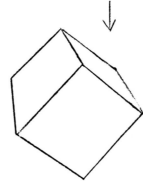

Divide a rectangle into four or five equal parts. Fold on dotted lines and lap a over b to form a three- or four-sided figure as below.

Cut on dotted line of square and lap a over b.

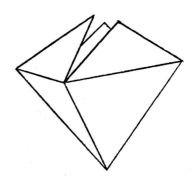

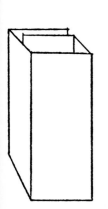
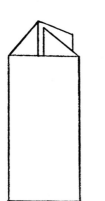

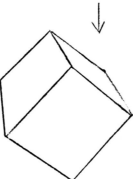

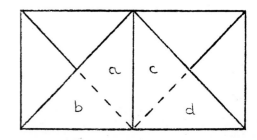

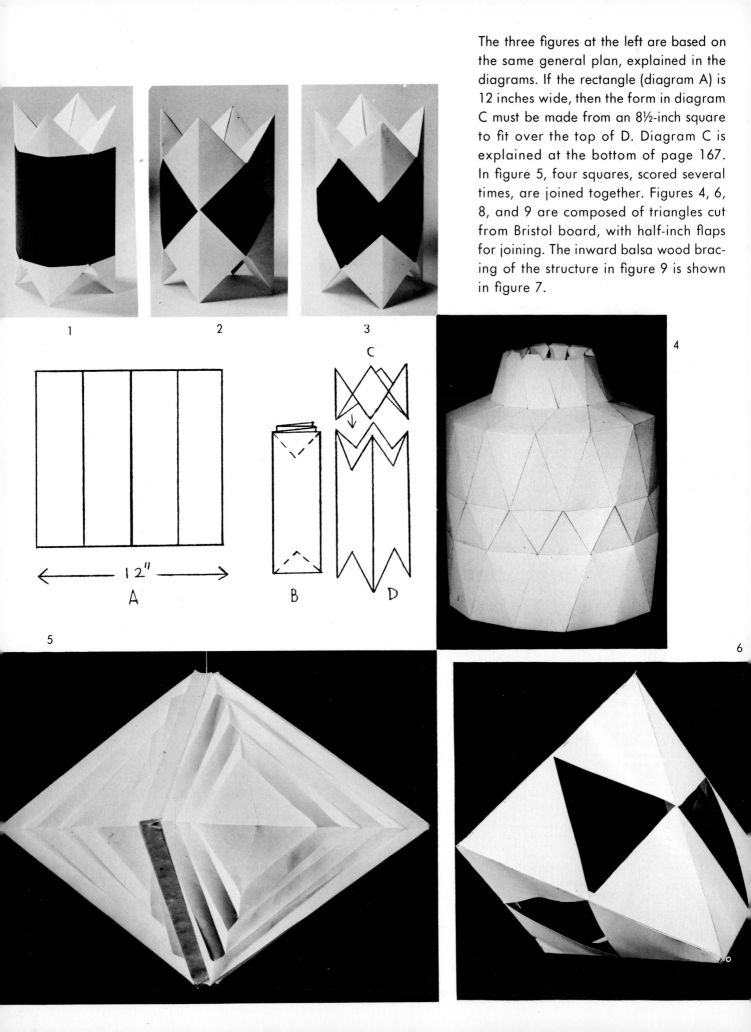

The three figures at the left are based on the same general plan, explained in the diagrams. If the rectangle (diagram A) is 12 inches wide, then the form in diagram C must be made from an 8½-inch square to fit over the top of D. Diagram C is explained at the bottom of page 167. In figure 5, four squares, scored several times, are joined together. Figures 4, 6, 8, and 9 are composed of triangles cut from Bristol board, with half-inch flaps for joining. The inward balsa wood bracing of the structure in figure 9 is shown in figure 7.

1

2

3

C

12"

A

B

D

4

5

6

7

9

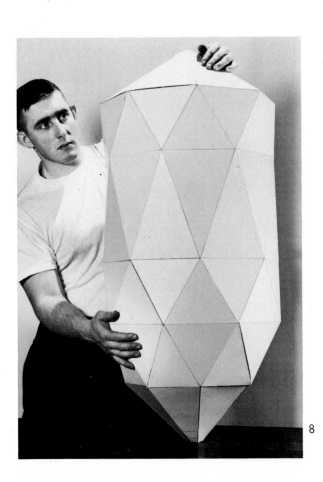

8

73

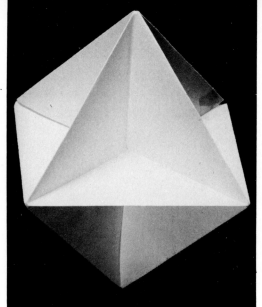

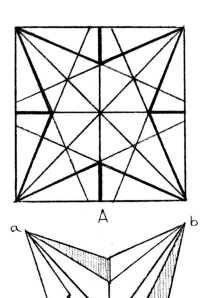

A

B

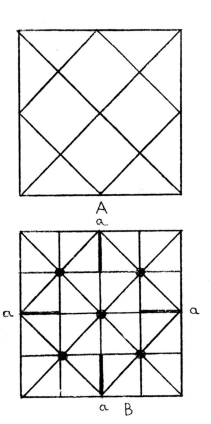

A

a

a   a

a   B

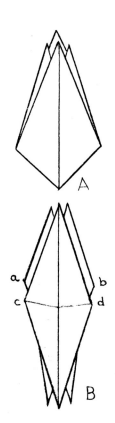

A

a   b

c   d

B

For the German bell above, follow the directions on page 148 through the fifth step, emphasizing the creases indicated in diagram A, above. Bend the creases so that the paper looks like diagram B. Gently pull upward the four outer points, a, b, c, d, until they meet. Fasten the points.

Fold a square along both diagonals. Then fold each corner to the center, creasing well. Turn the paper over and fold in half vertically and horizontally. Fold each edge to the center, forming sixteen squares. Crease well. Do not turn the paper over again. Cut on the heavy lines from the points marked a. Pop up the points indicated by the dots in diagram B and shape gently in the hands.

Follow the directions for folding the bird on page 148 through step 11. The results will be like diagrams A and B, above. Bend out the points a, b, c, and d so that a three-dimensional shape is formed. Tape together the points meeting at top and bottom and suspend on a thread.

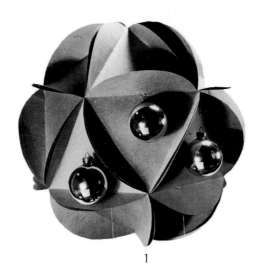

1

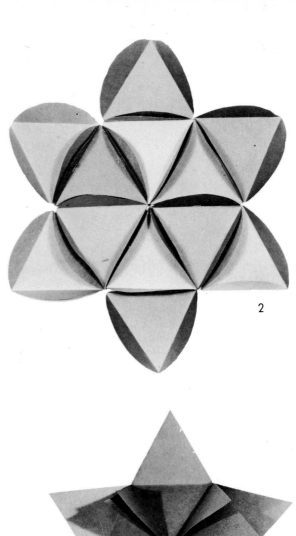

2

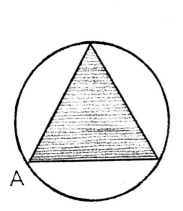

A

Cut a triangle from cardboard. Lay it on a cutout circle and trace around it. Trace the triangle on twenty circles.

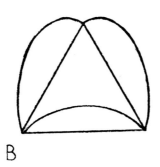

B

Crease the three traced lines on each circle and fold the three flaps upward.

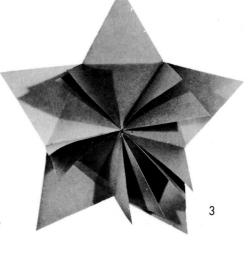

3

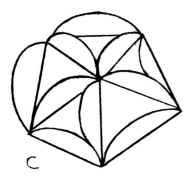

C

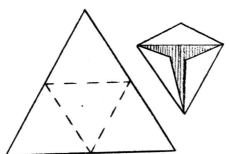

D

Staple or paste the flaps on five circles together to form the top of the ball. Use fifteen more to form the rest of the ball as in figure 1; or fasten together twelve circles to form a flat decorative pattern as in figure 2.

Try using triangles in place of circles, or try other variations to form balls and flat forms as shown in figures 3 and 4. Vary the colors or add paint for decoration.

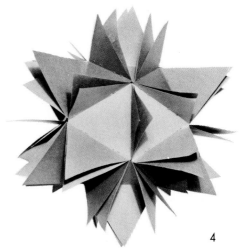

4

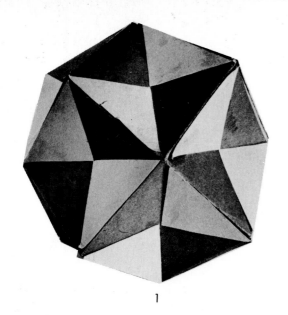

1

The many-sided polyhedron is structurally well suited for decoration because of the angular, repetitive nature of the form. It can be made of papers like colored construction, decorated with paint, crayon, or cut paper applied to the surface facets. For the structure in figure 1, a square sheet is folded into sixteen squares (diagram A), turned over, and diagonally folded from corner to corner (solid lines in diagram B). The corners are then folded individually to the center, and the four sides clipped at *ab*. The five points of intersection (dark spots) become the outside points and are popped up from underneath. The paper then falls easily into a ball, with the horizontal-vertical lines the "mountain" creases, and the diagonals, the "valley" creases. For stability, a second polyhedron pockets the first (figure 3) and is secured with tape or paste at the opening.

2

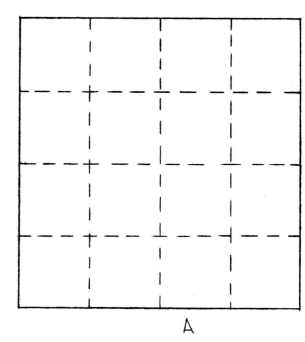

A

3

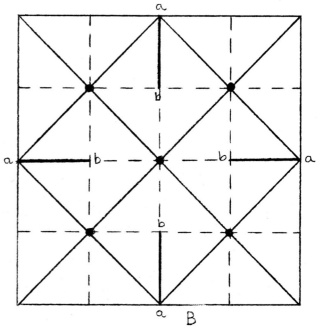

B

BUILDING FORMS

1

2

3

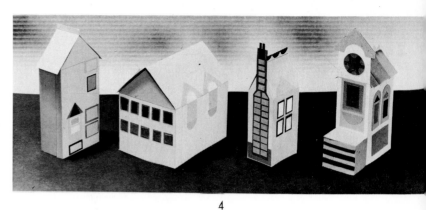

4

Geometric shapes are the basis of small building models like those shown on these pages. Variety is achieved through modifications of size and proportion and in the surface decoration. The diagrams give plans for basic structures, to which cones, cubes, and cylinders, already explained elsewhere, are added for the castle and other buildings. Compositions like the groupings of buildings and trees in figures 6 and 7 can be used for table decorations or employed in community study of a street or village in a classroom unit.

5

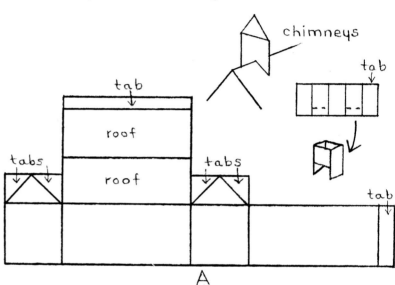

chimneys

tab

roof

roof

tabs

tabs

tab

tab

A

6

7

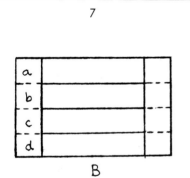

B

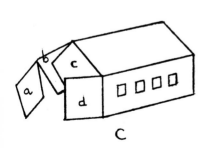

C

8

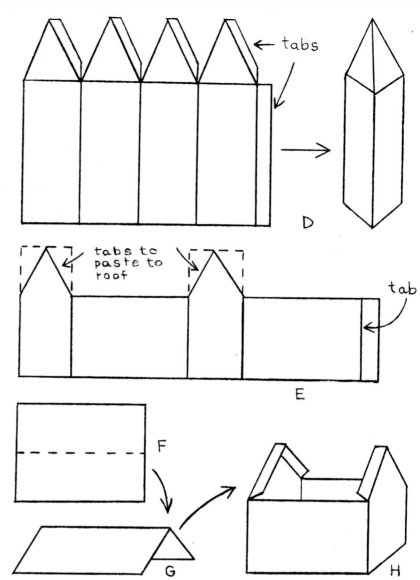

tabs

D

tabs to paste to roof

tab

E

F

G

H

9

1

CAGES AND BLOCKS

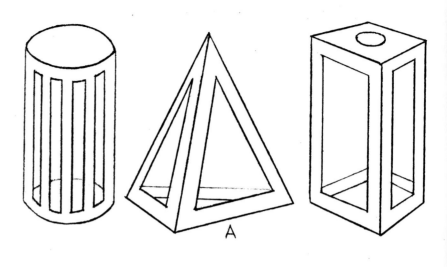

A

Lanterns and cages for festive occasions or other uses can be formed of basic shapes like the cube, cylinder, and various polyhedrons. The lantern in figure 1, made of colored construction papers with colored tissue paper inserts, is constructed from six sections, each composed of parts a and b (diagram B), held together with tabs.

Diagram C shows a form flat on the base and pointed on top that can be projected from a square or circle and have any desired number of sides. The triangular points at the ends are added, along with tabs for overlapping and pasting. Another lantern or cage structure is made of continuous sections joined together as in diagram D. For the shapes in diagram A see pages 41 and 70.

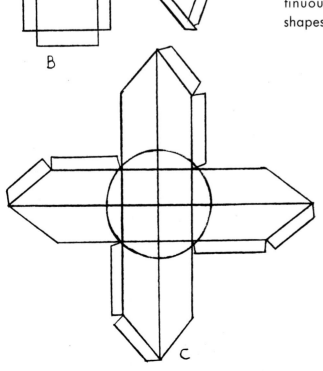

B

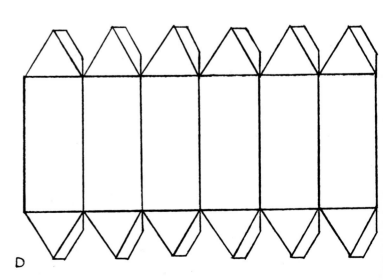

C   D

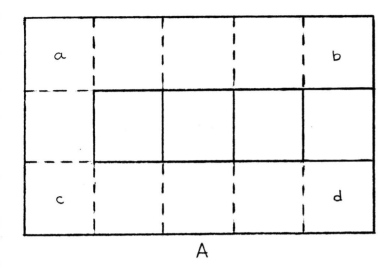

A

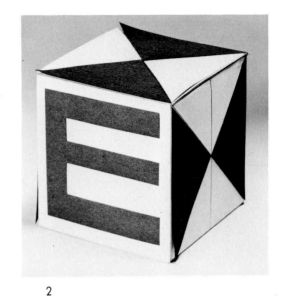

2

The cube or other six-sided block is the basis for a child's toy, a gift box, and other structures. Lightweight colored construction paper is good for small blocks, which can be decorated with paint or cut paper (figure 2). Larger blocks can be made of tag board, Bristol board, or chipboard (figure 3).

The cube in diagram A is made from a plan starting with fifteen squares in which the dotted lines are cut and sections a and c removed. When all the lines are creased, the shape can be assembled and pasted.

If cardboard is used, each of the six sides can be cut separately and held together with masking tape or gummed paper. The child's toy box in figure 1 is embellished with a delightful design cut from paper, showing forceful contrast of dark and light values in the adaptation of the vigorous animal shapes to the space.

1

3

1

2

W.A.A. SPECIAL

SPOKANE TRANSIT

3

The structures on these pages were designed and constructed by high school students, with the exception of the transportation models in figure 4, which were executed for luncheon table decorations by junior high school children. These students worked out their own plans; however, a suggestion is given in diagram A to show how a basic structure can be developed for such forms.

The example in figure 1 is constructed of lightweight cardboard, colored papers, and paper straws, with fringe around the top of the surrey. In figure 2 the base shape and fenders are cut from one piece of lightweight cardboard and covered with colored construction paper, which is also used for the body and engine of the car. The wheels are cardboard shapes connected with paper straw rods. Figure 3 has a balsa wood base with lightweight cardboard used for the body. Two sheets of colored construction paper, glued together for strength and pliability and shaped, form the roof. Glue and pins hold parts together, with the support of paper straws.

The bandstand in figure 5 is a six-sided figure reinforced underneath for strength. The musicians inside are supported with pipecleaners, which help achieve a feeling of action.

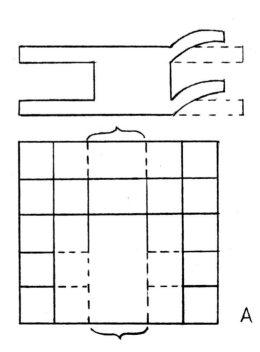

A

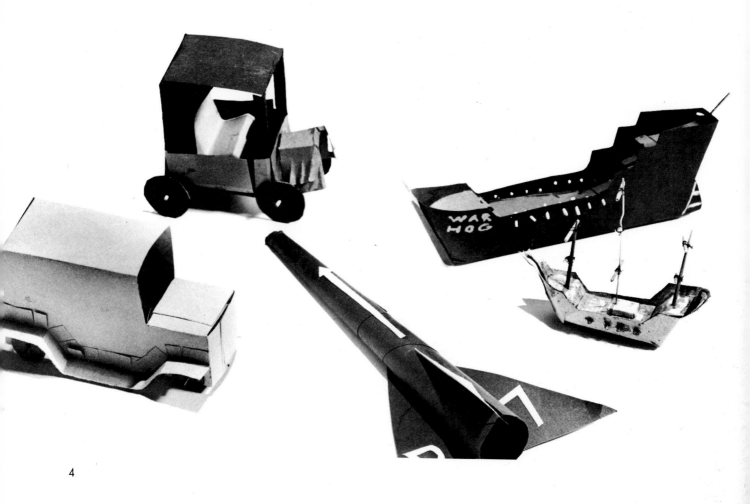

4

5

6

MOVING FORMS

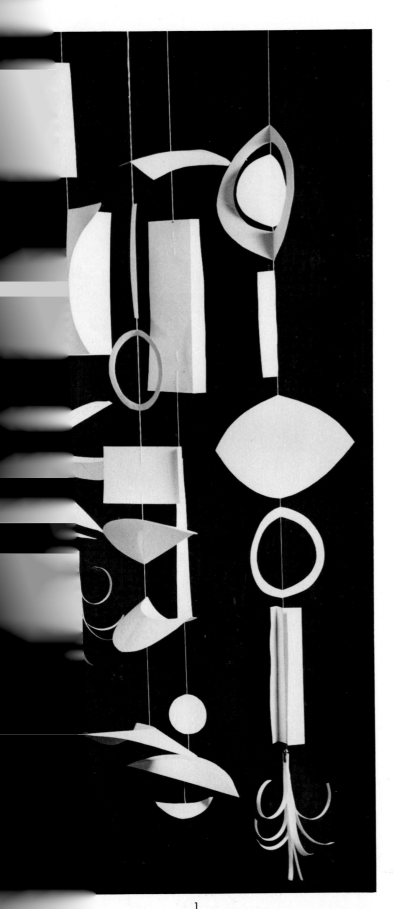

Exciting effects are produced by the interplay of shape and movement with suspended forms of paper or cardboard. Considerable adjusting and maneuvering are required in order to achieve balanced relationships. The forms are attached with threads to structures of balsa wood, wire, or cardboard (diagram B).

Approaches for constructing three-dimensional structures are shown in diagram A. Try various arrangements with paper strips as beginning experiments (a and b). Slits and staples help to hold the shapes in position. Turn the forms around to study their design and organization from various points of view.

Other pleasing forms can be produced through modeling or shaping two identically cut pieces of medium-weight paper, such as water-color paper, pasted together. When dry, they will retain any position desired.

The hanging structures in figures 2 and 3 are examples of how related forms can be used. Figure 2 shows strips of paper stapled together. The forms of figure 3 are shown in diagram D and in figure 2 on page 47.

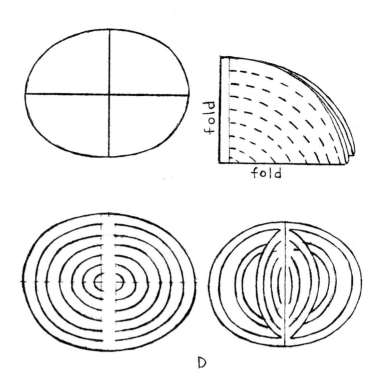

Start with a circle, oval, square, or other shape. Fold and cut from double fold edge as indicated at upper right, above.

2

Score an S shape and fold into pleats. Join ends.

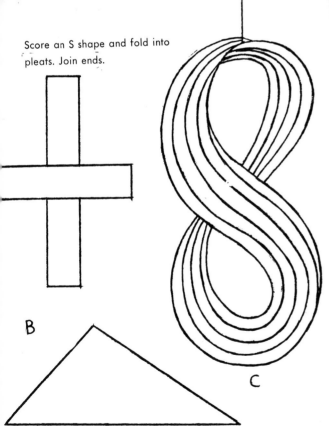

B

C

Cardboard structures for attaching mobile forms.

3

PLANES

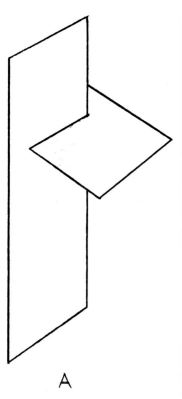

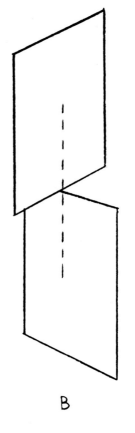

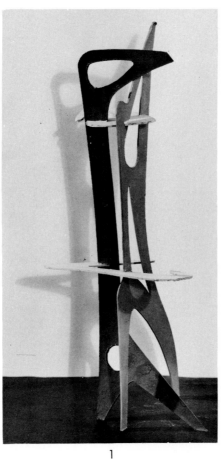

A

1

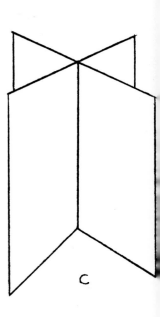

Cut on dotted lines and slip cards together at right angles.

B

C

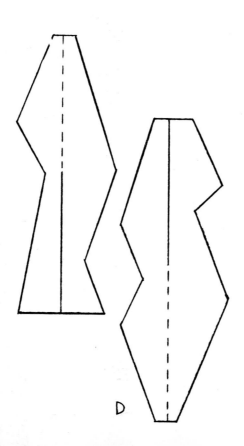

D

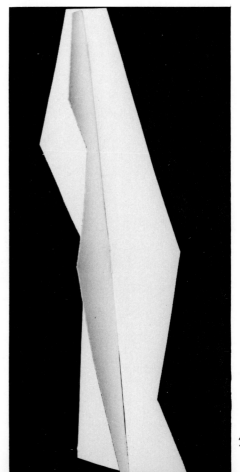

2

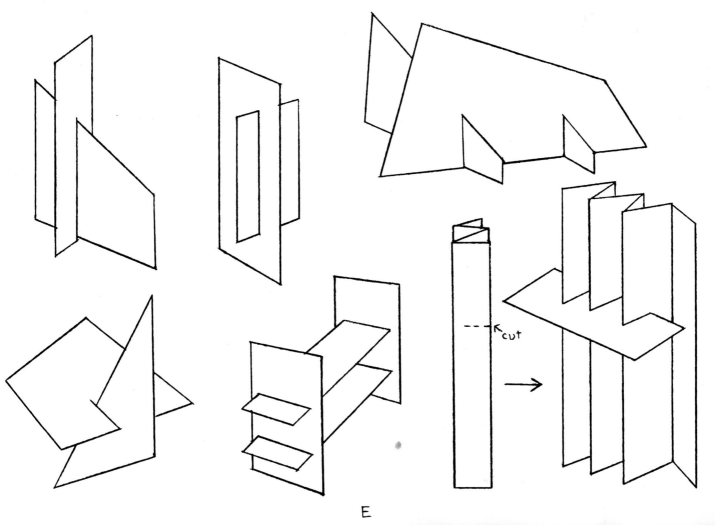

E

Planes are flat surfaces that can be related to other planes for creating movement and direction into space. A simple basic plane relationship can be demonstrated with two pieces of paper slit to the center and fitted together at right angles (diagrams B and C). For variation, the contours can be cut in related shapes as in figure 2, explained in diagram D. A more complex structure is shown in figure 1, made of cardboard with the added element of color in the painted surfaces. A pleasing sculptural quality is achieved in the relationship of the vertical cutout planes with the horizontal inserts (diagram A). A similar composition, showing two related vertical shapes interlocked with slits, can be seen on page 88. More ways of relating planes are suggested in diagram E, where the problem is to balance one shape with another. Flat cards with decorated surfaces are suspended on threads to produce a mobile construction of planes moving in space (figure 3).

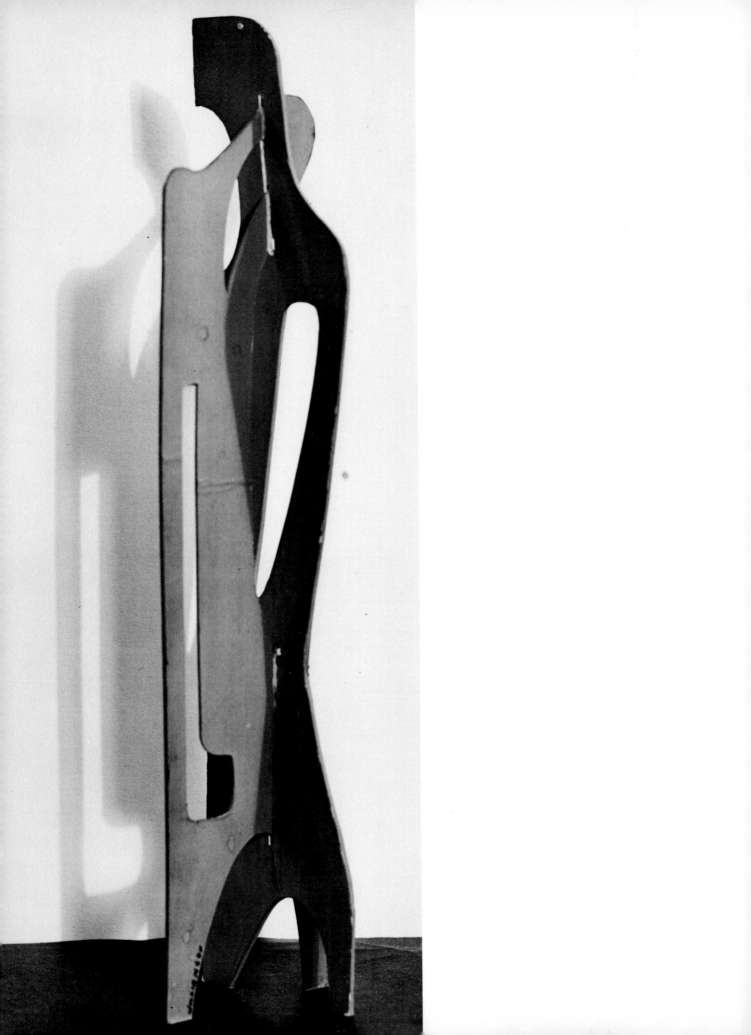

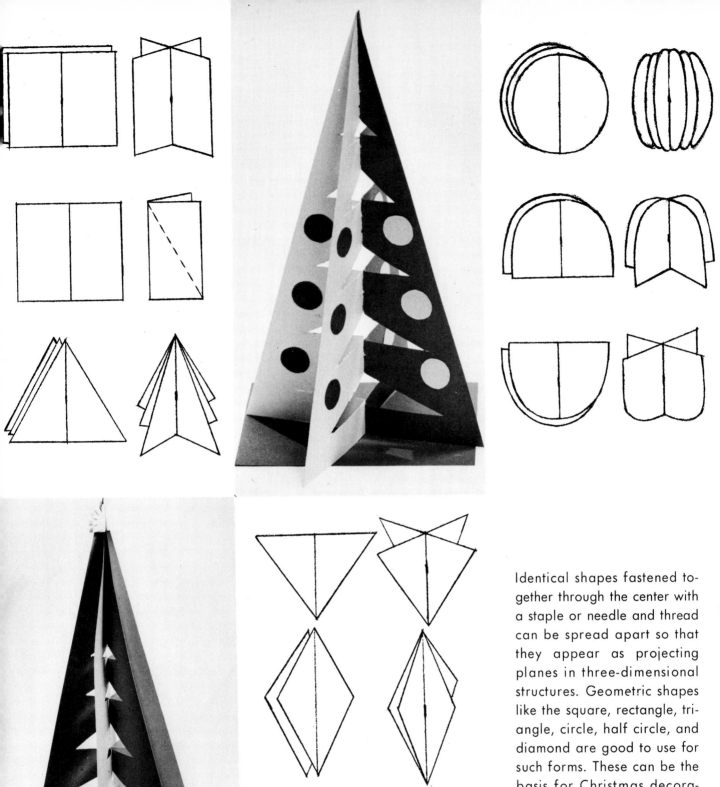

Identical shapes fastened together through the center with a staple or needle and thread can be spread apart so that they appear as projecting planes in three-dimensional structures. Geometric shapes like the square, rectangle, triangle, circle, half circle, and diamond are good to use for such forms. These can be the basis for Christmas decorations, gift cards, or favors. The butterfly on page 24, the egg on page 159, and the tree structures shown on this page are examples of the application of this principle.

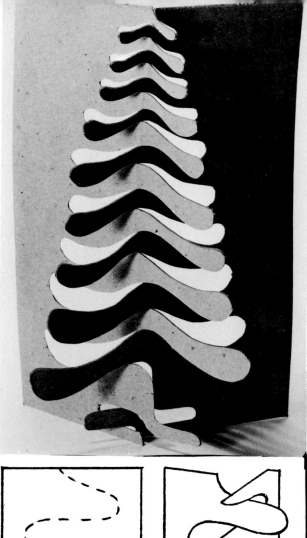

The tree form on the left is a splendid example of the use of interlocking planes produced by cutting a continuous line in a sheet of heavy paper or cardboard. This principle is explained in diagrams A, B, and C. The illustration in figure 2 shows another version of the problem. For the three-dimensional structures on the facing page, sections of the flat sheet of paper have been partly cut and bent outward. The projecting planes produce a sculptural effect through contrast of dark and light.

1

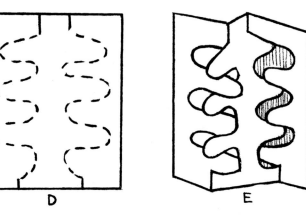

D   E

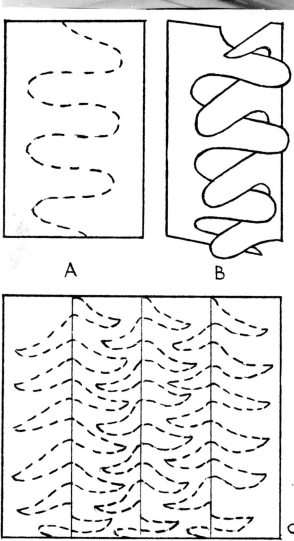

A   B

C

2

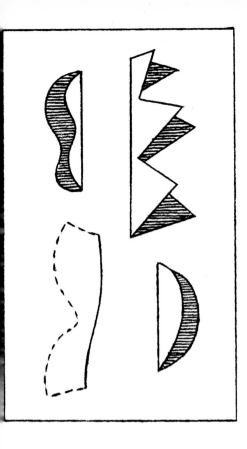

3

4

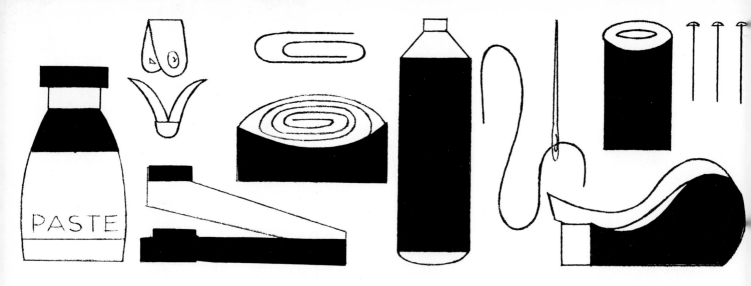

WAYS TO FASTEN THINGS TOGETHER

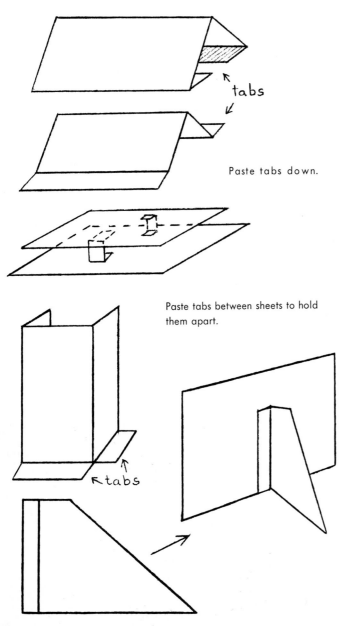

tabs

Paste tabs down.

Paste tabs between sheets to hold them apart.

tabs

There are a number of ways of attaching one piece of paper to another. Brads, pins, paper clips, needle and thread, and staples are among the mechanical means available. Tiny staplers are helpful for reaching into unusually small openings, while long staplers are advisable for more extensive spaces. An average size and a long stapler are shown on page 2. Sometimes it is more convenient to use pieces of tape, especially in inaccessible places where a stapler will not reach. Tape is handy for securing parts for temporary purposes or for expediency when working for quick results. A double-coated masking tape is also useful. Paper can be fastened by tabs, shown on this page, and slits, illustrated on the facing page. There are some very fine pastes and glues, and rubber cement is excellent for certain problems.

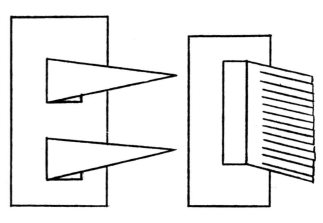

Bend paper to form tabs.

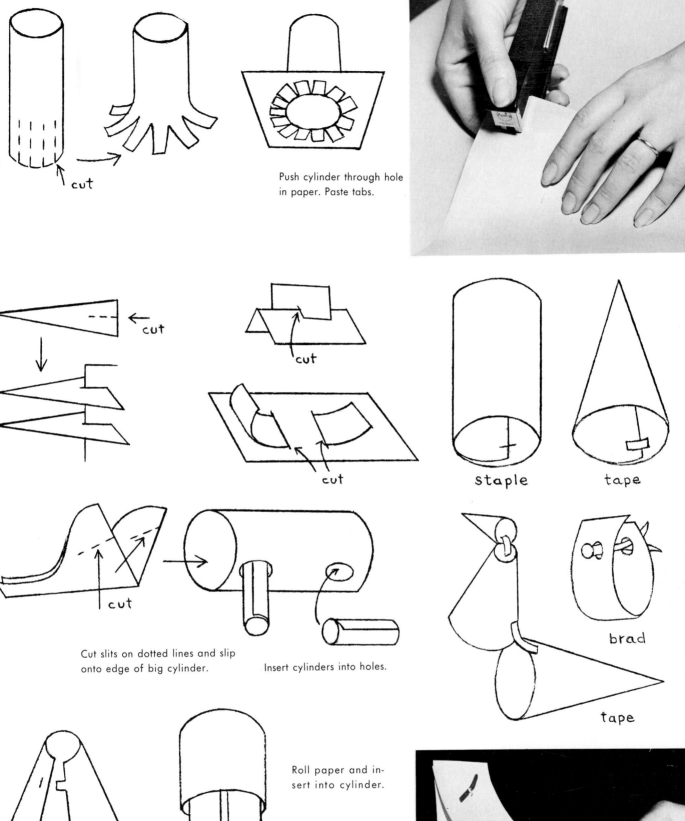

Push cylinder through hole
in paper. Paste tabs.

staple   tape

Cut slits on dotted lines and slip
onto edge of big cylinder.

Insert cylinders into holes.

brad

tape

Roll paper and in-
sert into cylinder.

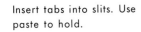

Insert tabs into slits. Use
paste to hold.

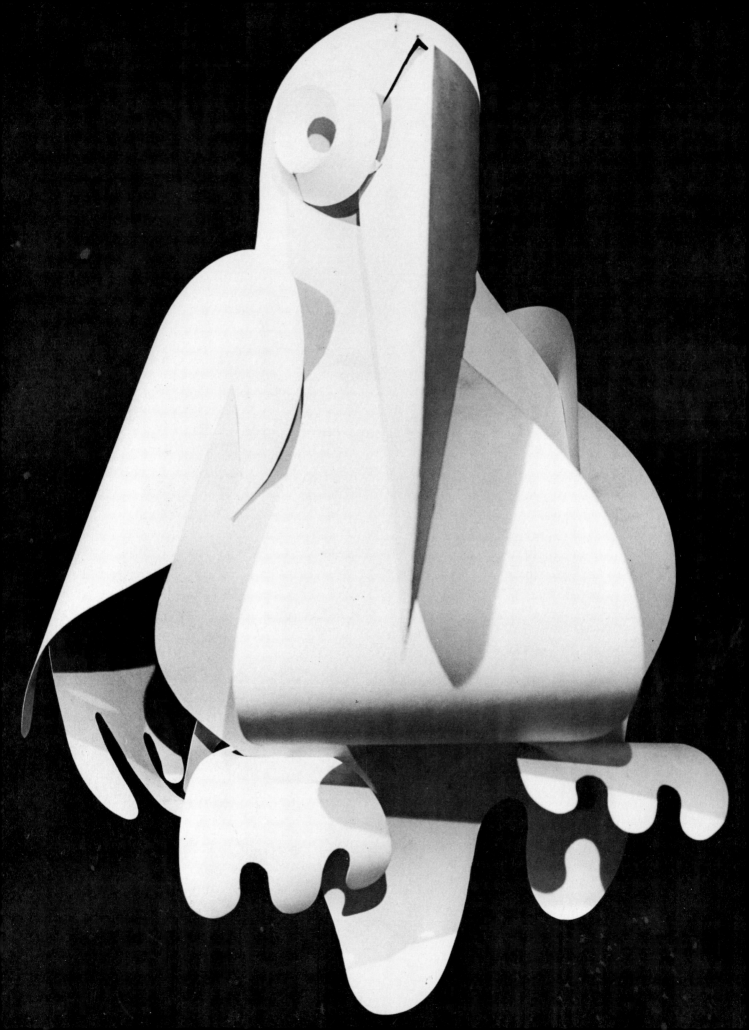

APPROACHES TO CREATING

Experience in working with paper and discovering its possibilities through cutting, curling, bending, shaping, scoring, constructing volumes, and relating planes helps in creating with this material. Shapes like strips, squares, rectangles, circles, cones, and cylinders are the basis for many structures, either alone or in combination with other shapes. The various techniques learned while exploring the potentials of paper can be used to advantage in working out creative solutions to problems. It is important to think in terms of the abstract qualities of the paper while working with it, as it is through sculptural form that esthetic values are realized and pleasure is derived.

The bird sculpture of white Bristol board in the photograph at the left was cut, scored, bent, curled, and assembled with paste, tape, interlocking slits, and brads. To get some idea of the shapes developed after much experimentation, the structure was taken apart and photographed (figure 2).

Approaches to creating are presented on the following pages as suggestions for a starting point in developing original ideas through working with the shapes and the materials.

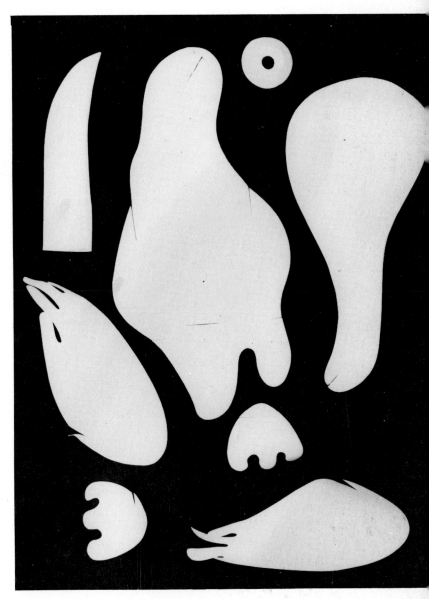

2

EXPERIMENTING WITH VARIOUS SHAPES

A variety of ideas can be developed with paper strips. A number are suggested here. For a good supply of material, save scraps from white and colored papers. Examples of how strips can be manipulated by looping, folding, bending, and curling are shown. From the suggestions given, more ideas can be developed after a little exploration with the shapes. To secure several strips together, a stapler or brad or paste will usually suffice. Many forms like these can be used for attractive, festive decorations for holidays and parties.

STRIPS

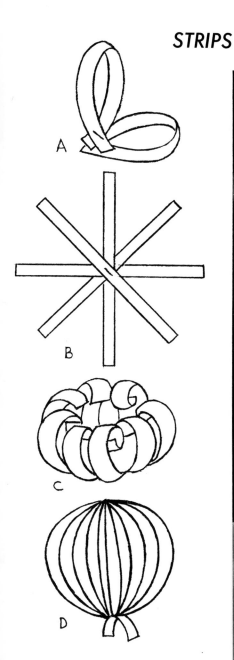

A

B

C

D

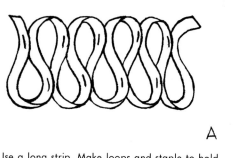

Use a long strip. Make loops and staple to hold.

A

B

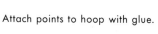

Attach points to hoop with glue.

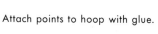

More structures developed from simple paper strips looped and folded in various ways are shown here. Some, like those in the photograph above, can be enjoyed for their abstract qualities alone, while others have a subject matter interest as well. The Halloween character in figure 2 was made by a child from a ball of paper strips with cut-paper pieces added for detail. The horse and rider of figure 3 were also made by a child.

The exquisite wands on page 100 have a fantasy quality exciting to the imagination of children or adults. Delicately proportioned and rhythmically planned in terms of color and form, they inspire a sensitivity for paper as an expressive material. A wood dowel stick is used as a support for the strips.

1

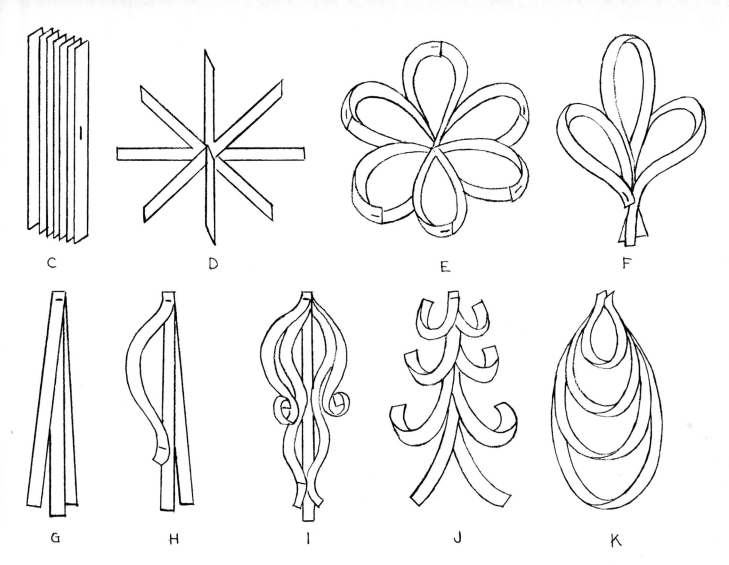

C   D   E   F

G   H   I   J   K

2

3

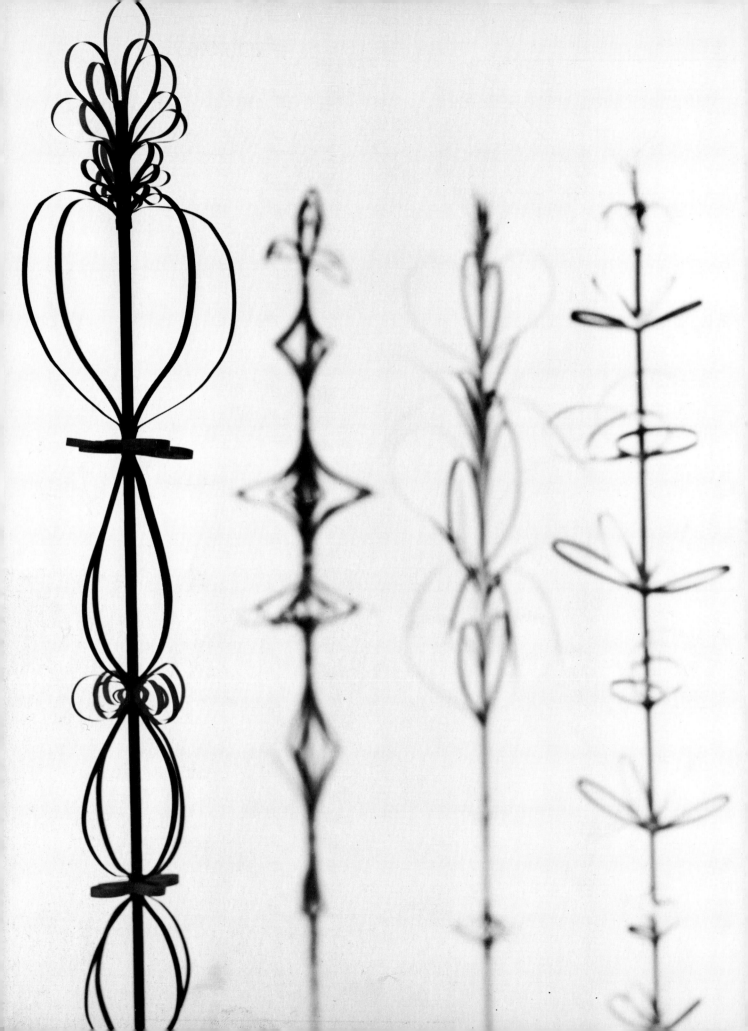

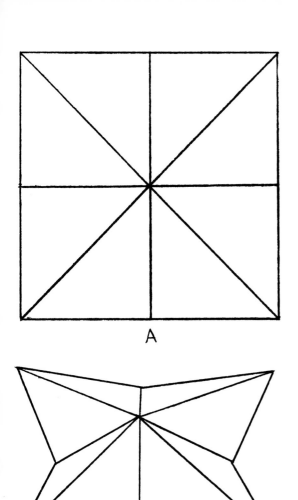

A

B

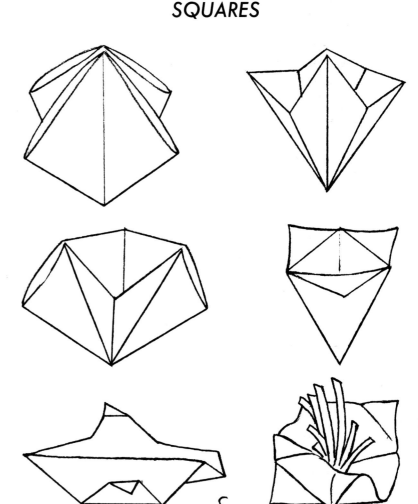

C

The square has been used in folk art as the foundation for many paper-folding problems, as shown in the traditional Japanese bird on page 148. The structural qualities of the square can be observed by creasing it in half in each direction, turning it over, and creasing it from corner to corner both ways. If the creases are sharp, the square shape can be maneuvered into various positions, a few of which are presented here. Many other ideas can be explored through bending, curling, cutting, scoring, and pleating the paper, but it is desirable to retain the feeling of the square shape as much as possible. To make the pinwheel, crease a square from corner to corner, cut from each corner almost to the center, bring every other corner to the center, and fasten with a brad or with paste.

1

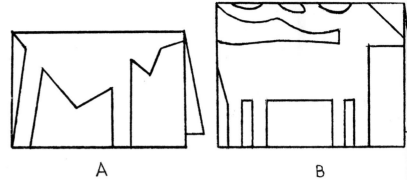

A

B

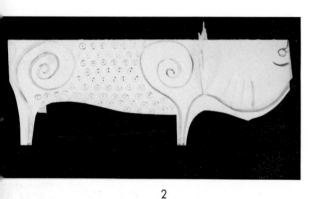

2

4

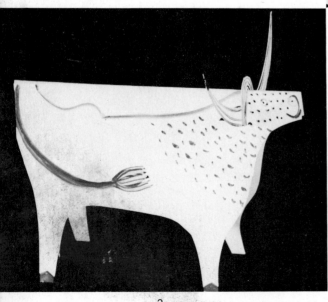

3

The animals here are made from rectangles, some folded with a crease on top and cut symmetrically to facilitate standing. Others are rounded without creasing as in figures 1 and 5, with a few areas of the paper cut out so that head, legs, and tail are suggested. The paper is overlapped beneath to hold the form together (figure 5). Additional parts are used in some of the structures, like the lion's mane, which is formed of a fringed strip, and the cut shapes of heads and horns, which have been inserted with slits. A reference to nature will strengthen concepts of animal design, supplying information needed for creating.

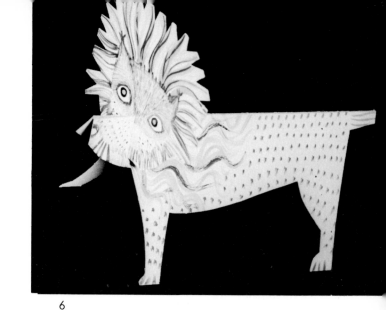

5

6

C

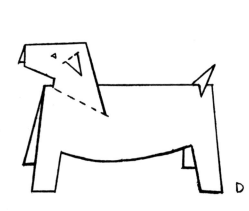

D

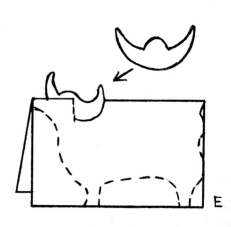

E

7

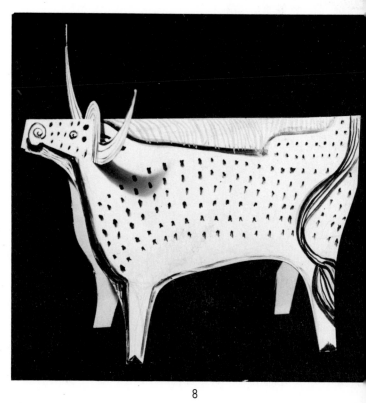

8

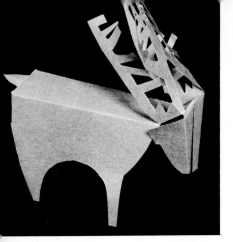
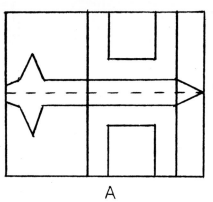

A

B

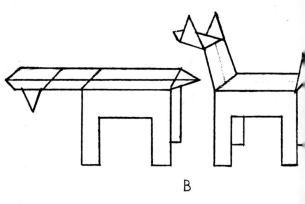

The animals on this page are constructed from rectangles folded with a flat section on top, as explained in diagram A. The space is divided so that a narrow strip forms the back along which the head, ears, neck, and tail are indicated. The legs and sides of the body are shaped by cutting out unneeded portions, after which the structure is bent so that it will stand up. The characteristic parts of animals can be suggested and simplified with emphasis on the sculptural qualities of the paper rather than upon imitation of natural forms.

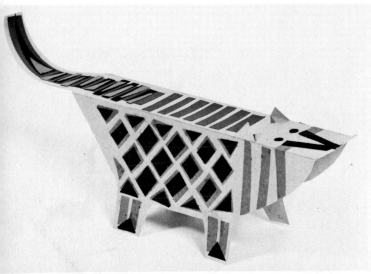

Folded structures that stand upright are another type of foundation that can be used for animals. Small ones made of colored construction or lightweight papers can serve as place cards or table and tray favors. For construction of very large forms, stronger papers like cardboard or other heavier types are needed. These structures can be made with a crease down the center of the back or with a flat plane like the animals described on the opposite page. Characteristic parts like the head, ears, legs, and other identifying features need to be considered, and the legs should be made wide enough to support the animal so that it will stand up without difficulty.

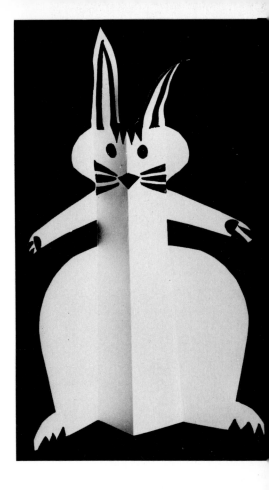

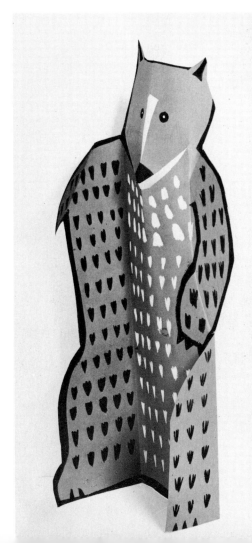

CONES

1

2

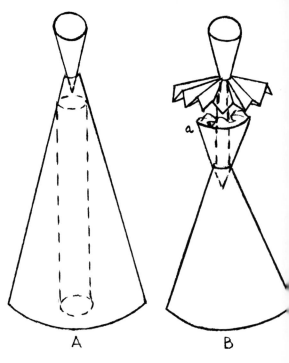

Cones can be attached to each other with glue or tape. The cone a in diagram B is crushed inward at the top to help support the cylinder attached to the head cone. This principle was used in figure 3.

The cone is an adaptable form with which to work. Here it is used for the construction of human figures. It can be applied to a skirt, trousers, sleeves, a part of a hat, or, inverted, the bodice of a dress. These suggestions may help in giving direction to ideas. Other shapes, for example the cylinder or the cube, can be used successfully in combination with the cone.

If it is necessary to give a structure more support, a cardboard tube or cylinder of paper put underneath the cone will provide stability. Figures 1 and 2 are enhanced by the responsive quality of the butcher paper used; the rest of the examples shown are formed of colored construction papers. The skater and the dancer were made by children for table decorations, with cones of various widths serving a variety of purposes. The one forming the body of the wise man in figure 6 is less than a fourth of a circle. The head was built on the top of the cone, which can be seen emerging through the crown, and pieces of scrap papers were added to form the features and other parts. When features are used, they should contribute to the decorative quality of the structure and be part of the total design.

3

4

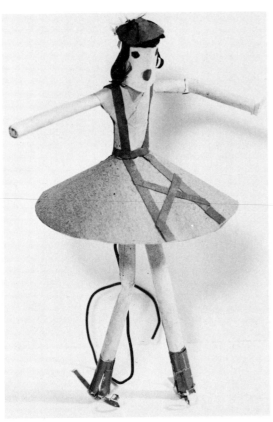

5

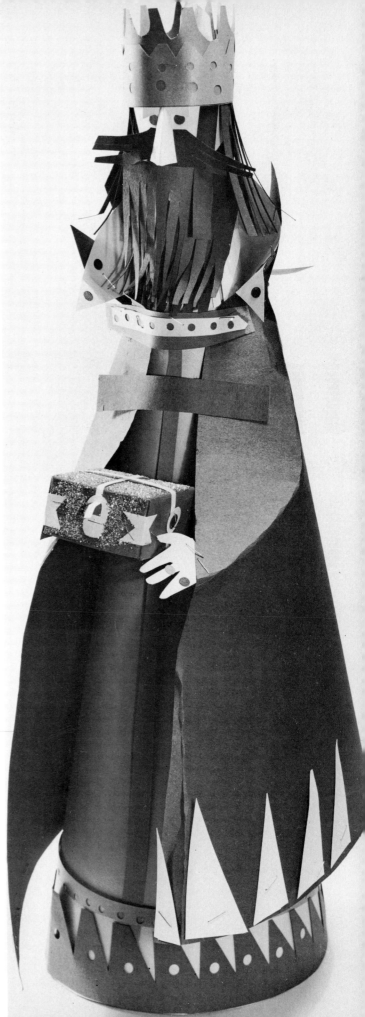

6

Cut on dotted lines. Lap flap a over b, and flap c over d, to form a boxlike top for a figure.

After fastening the sides, insert a long roll of paper through the opening to suggest arms, as in figures 4 and 5 on the preceding page; or form arms of flat paper as in figure 2 on the facing page.

1

2

A

B

C

D

E

F

G

+ H

= I

J

HEADS

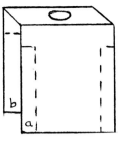
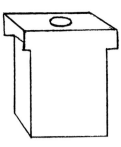

Cut folded structure on dotted lines. Fold and lap *a* over *b*. Do the same to the other side. This makes a boxlike top suggestive of shoulders for a military effect.

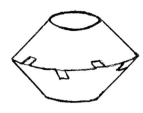

Inverted cones make a hip structure.

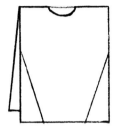

Fold on diagonal lines and overlap on each side to form a bodice. Add other parts to build out a figure structure.

2

3

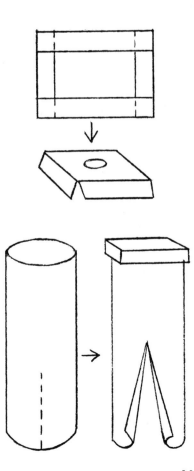

109

CIRCLES

Simple flower forms can be made from a basic circle shape. Experiments in cutting petals and leaves will help to develop a variety of ideas. When the circle is cut from the outside edge to the center and rolled with the center as a pivot, a pleasing form results (diagram A). From folded circles, petals can be cut and then creased, scored, or curled. When the circle is cut from the outer edge to the center and the edges are slightly overlapped, a three-dimensional conelike form is produced.

Leaf shapes can also be scored for a three-dimensional effect. Examples of their use can be seen in the decorative tree on page 188. For greater depth, one end can be slit and the slit edges overlapped.

In the photograph on the facing page are shown structures made from butcher paper following the plans given in the diagrams. Here, again, beauty of form is emphasized rather than literal imitation of nature.

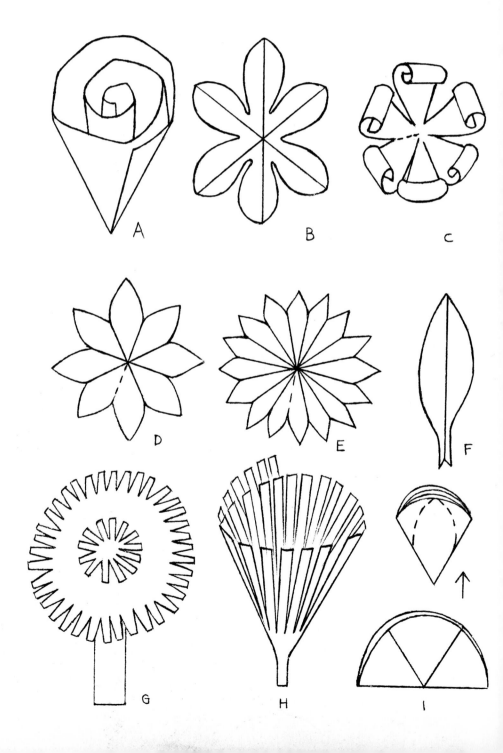

1

2

Several cylinders assembled in interesting relationships and proportions result in a pleasing composition. The soldier is built almost entirely of cylinders with the legs formed according to the plan at the bottom of page 93. Figure 2 could be either a king or a wise man. The lamb is made of cylinders and covered with fringed, curled strips (see diagram B, page 39).

3

HOLIDAYS

CHRISTMAS TREES

Christmas trees, a festive addition to the holiday table, can be made of colored construction, metallic, tissue, or other interesting papers. Those shown here are shaped of cones or built upon cylindrical structures. A mailing tube is sufficient support (figure 3), or a pole can be constructed by rolling a sheet of paper. Figures 1, 2, and 5 are built upon cones; figure 4 is constructed according to one of the cutout plans on page 20.

1

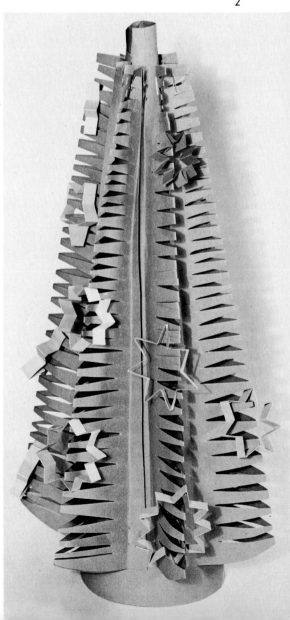

2

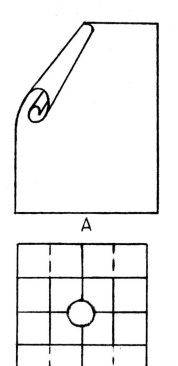

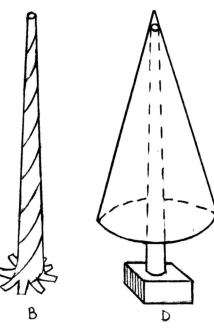

A

C

B

D

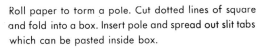

Roll paper to form a pole. Cut dotted lines of square and fold into a box. Insert pole and spread out slit tabs which can be pasted inside box.

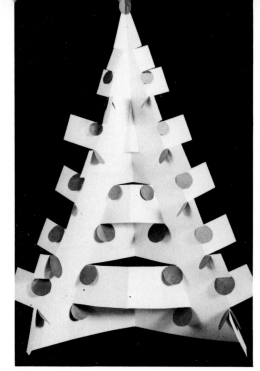

4

3

5

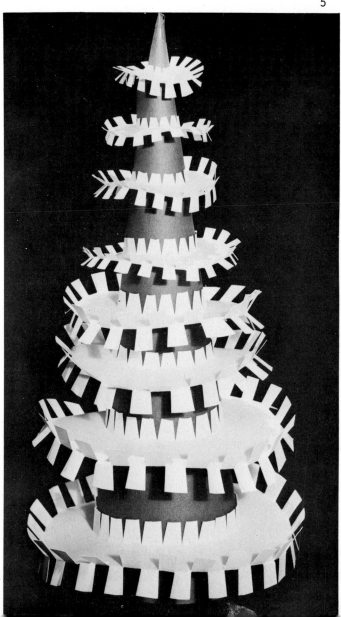

ANGEL DESIGNS

Angels are delightful forms through which enchantment is added to holiday decorations. Gay and colorful or restrained and dignified, they can be made of white paper, gold or colored metal foil, colored papers, or other materials to serve as diminutive tree decorations, folded Christmas cards, stately table and mantel decorations, church decorations, or store window displays. The addition of sequins, tinsel, sparkle, or paint contributes to the decorative quality of the structures. The angel in figure 1 is made of a rectangle with the head, wings, and body all cut from one sheet of paper. The arms are added after being scored down the center. The circle halo and the hair are formed of curled strips.

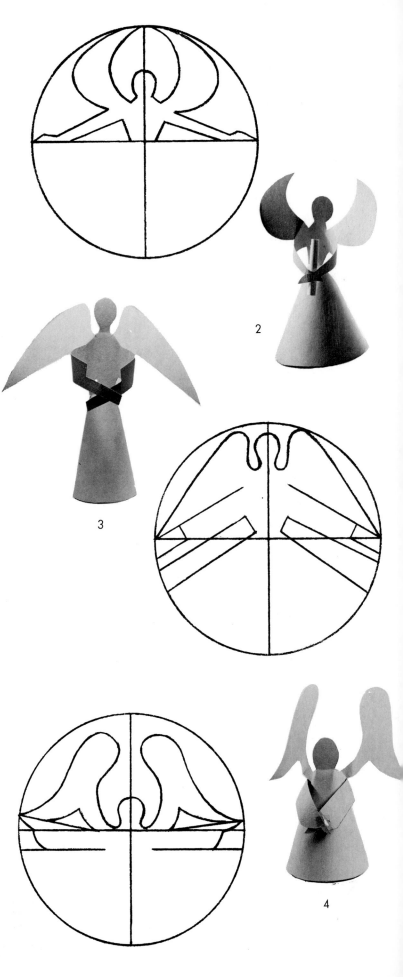

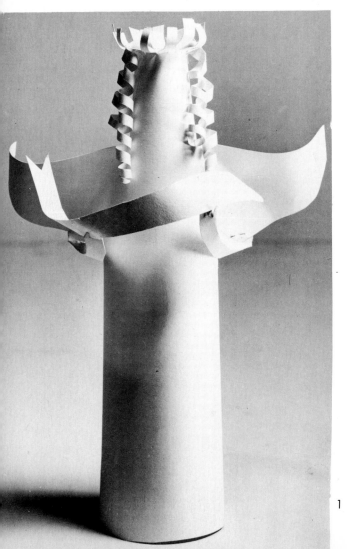

1

2

3

4

A simple way to construct an angel is shown in the lower right-hand corner of the page. Half of the figure is drawn along the edge of a folded piece of paper and cut out. Wings, also cut along the fold, can be long or short, wide or narrow, upward or downward in direction. Such additions as a varied edge, textured surface, or scored lines might be considered for detail interest.

Angels constructed in a circle can be cut all in one piece. Establish guides for planning the figure by drawing a vertical line through the center and a horizontal one at right angles to it. Figures 2, 3, 4, 5, and 6 show a number of possibilities and indicate how the angel looks when rounded and fastened together to stand. It is important in shaping the skirt to make the figure balance so that it will not tip over. The examples presented all function satisfactorily.

The form in figure 7 is built upon a cone-shaped structure with pointed tabs projecting from the sides. The flat treatment of the head and face helps to emphasize design qualities.

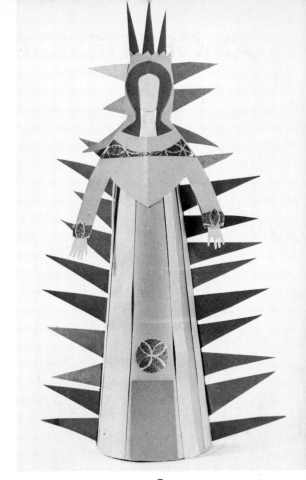

7

5

6

117

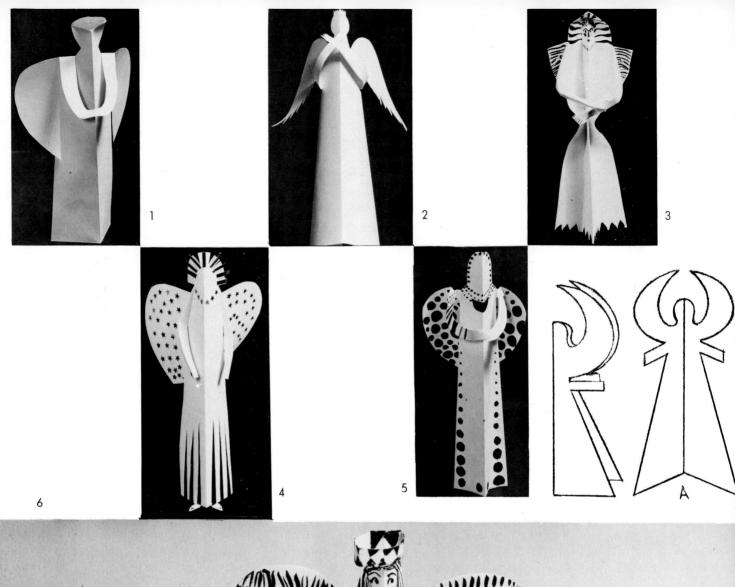

Angels are beautiful as festive decorations. They can be cut from cardboard, left flat, and decorated, and then suspended by threads from a ceiling fixture like the group hanging from a cardboard star in figure 7. For a row of angels joined together to group around a chandelier or use for a table centerpiece (figure 8), trace half of the shape on a folded strip of paper and cut (diagram B). Several such sections can be cut and joined together to make a longer strip. The angels on the facing page are cut in one piece from a folded sheet of paper (diagram A). Many different papers can be used. Metallic papers have a gay look, and angels of colored cellophane are effective when taped on the window pane. Cardboard angels can be used on a mantel, in a church foyer, or for a crèche.

7

8

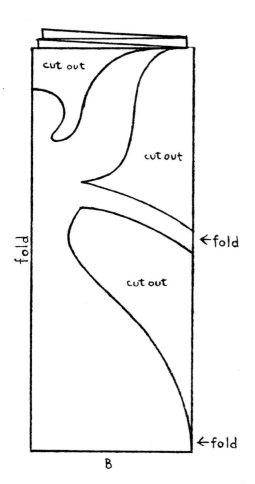

cut out

cut out

fold

←fold

cut out

←fold

B

1

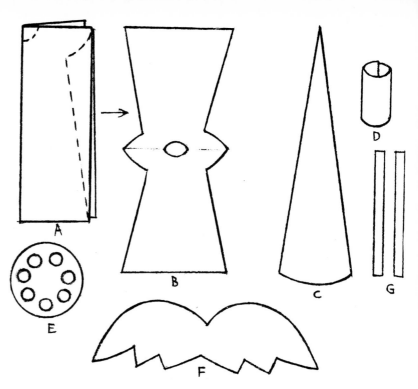

The angel in figure 1 is based on a cone cut from a quarter circle. Over this is put a shape like B, diagramed in A. A cylinder can be slipped over the top of the cone for a head, and a halo decorated with perforations, cut paper, or sequins can be attached with tape. Wings are cut folded and attached with tape to the back, and paper strips serve as arms.

2

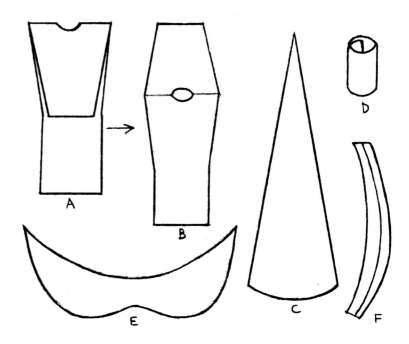

The angel in figure 2 is made of a cone cut from a quarter circle. Over this is placed a shape like that diagramed in A and B. This bodice has a long section in back which is folded up and used as a support in which to encase the wings. The wings are cut from folded paper, and the arms are cut and scored down the center for a three-dimensional effect.

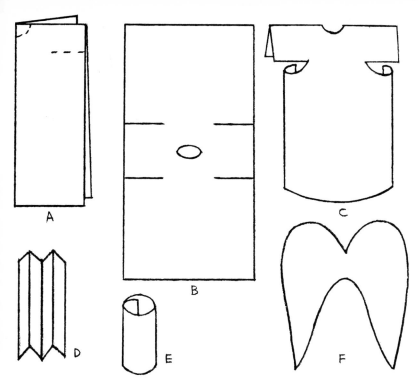

The body for figure 3 is made by folding a sheet of paper in half vertically and horizontally as in A and cutting on the dotted lines. Opened up, the paper looks like B. When shaped as in C, the shoulders become arms and the front of the skirt wraps around over the back and is secured with tape or paste. A cylinder head is inserted through the hole for the neck, and the wings are taped to the back. A folded paper, D, can be attached to the skirt.

3

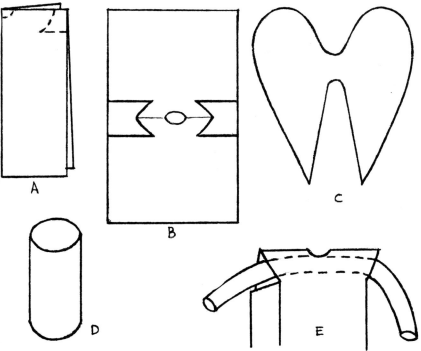

In figure 4 the body is shaped from a structure cut as in A and B. Arms are inserted through the openings in the shoulders, and a cylinder head is attached to the arms through the neck opening. Wings are taped to the back. Additional interest can be achieved through detail on skirt, wings, or crown.

4

1

2

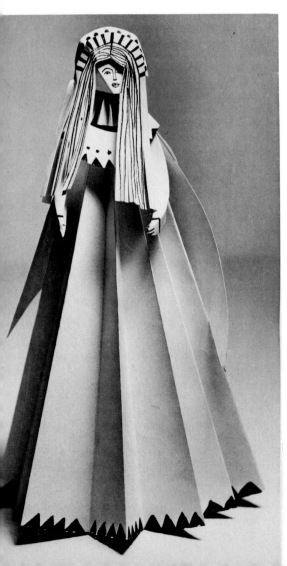

3

Angel structures made of several parts fitted together are shown here. The cone is used as a foundation for figure 1; the other two examples are made of pleated rectangles. The angel on the facing page is made of white construction paper and is semiround, to fit against a flat wall surface. Scored lines help make the figure rounded and sculptural. If a pattern is cut of butcher or other paper, proportions can be worked out and parts related together in advance.

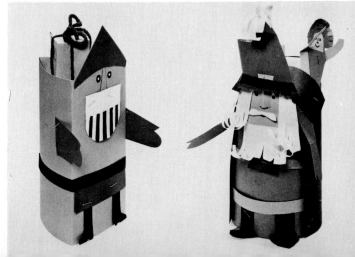

1

2

3

4

5

6

SANTA CLAUS

The traditional figure of Santa Claus can be the source for many imaginative creations if design elements are kept in mind and sculptural form considered. The examples shown here are made of colored construction papers, employing primarily cylinders and cones for the basic structure. The example in figure 3 is built upon an inverted paper cup. The two examples in figure 6, creased so that they are flat in front and rounded in back, are made to hold toy favors in the opening created behind.

The reindeer in the photograph above is cut from paper with the folded edge on top enabling it to stand. More examples of this type of structure will be found on page 102.

CHRISTMAS DECORATIONS

The Christmas season provides many occasions for sharing happy experiences. Trimming the tree and making decorations offer unlimited opportunities to create inspired designs. Delightful papers, varied in color and texture, like tissue paper, cellophane, Oriental papers, and metallic-surfaced ones, are stimulating to work with, and the addition of paint, glitter, and sequins serves to enhance the decorative and festive qualities.

Traditional forms, universal in appeal, can often be used in original ways. For example, the enchanting pattern of the paper chain on the opposite page is produced by repeating the units of simple looped strips, but variety is added by changing the width or length of the strips, or by using metallic papers and gay combinations of colors.

The Christmas tree is a dramatic spectacle when thought is given to the selection of pleasing forms and color relationships. There are many structures in this book, including both pure forms and those derived from nature, like birds or stars, that are suitable for adaptation as tree decorations.

On page 129 a tree is shown decorated with only one type of ornament. The paper ball is made of some thin paper like onionskin, tissue paper, or a bond paper. Sometimes it is effective to limit the decorative units to two or three types of structures. If too many different items are used, the effect may be confused and lacking in organization.

Many families find common enjoyment in sharing together the making of trimmings and other types of decorations. Children especially are thrilled with the delightful creations they are able to construct. Simple structures that even a small child can produce are suggested on pages 130 and 131. Much fun can be had in developing ideas and trying out various possibilities. Often more value and pleasure are gained through this type of experience than from purchasing something already made.

Other forms of ornament are shown on the following pages. All will be helpful as suggestions for constructing innumerable figures. Some can be used in windows; others on the fireplace, suspended from the ceiling or a light fixture, on a table, or on a door. The results can be very impressive if the objects are made large in scale and striking in color.

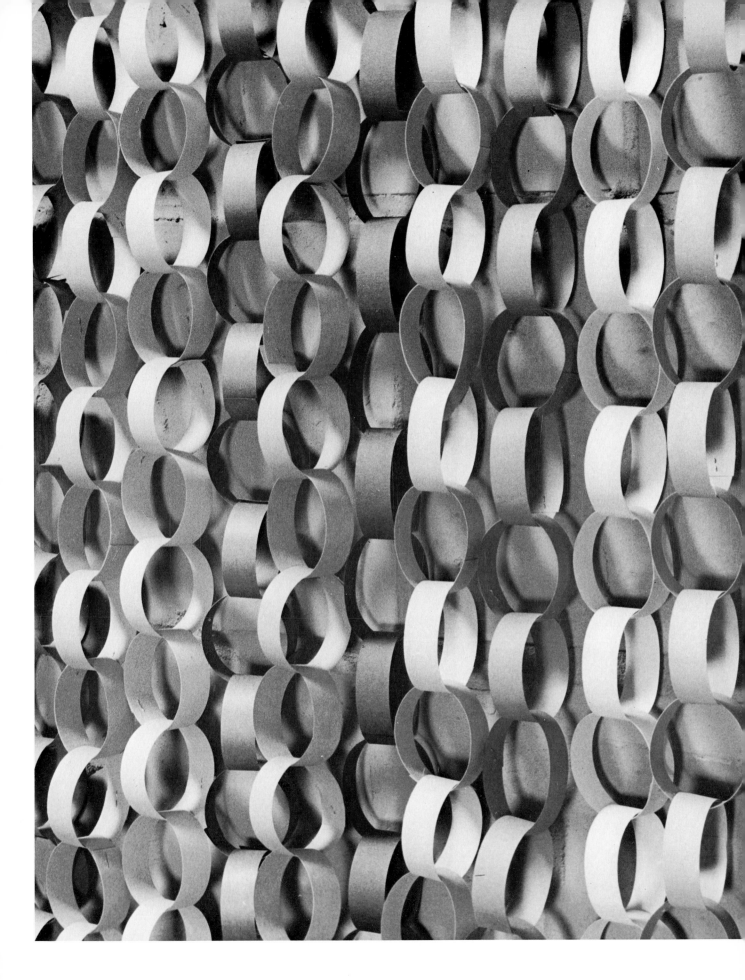

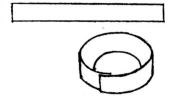

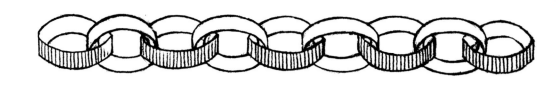

Vary paper strips in color, width, and length. Try construction and metallic papers.

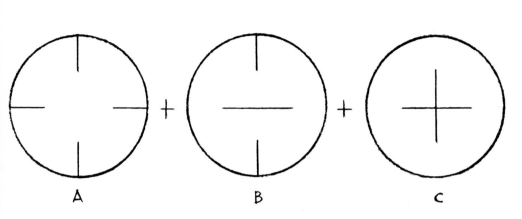

Cut lines in each of the three circles. Fold A in half and insert through center of B. Open up A. Fold A and B and insert through center of C, forming interlocking ball as in D.

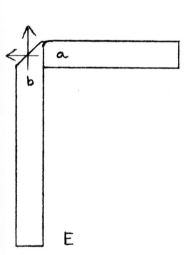

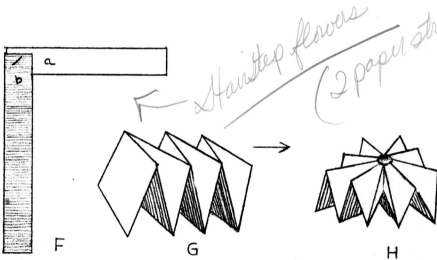

Stairstep flowers (2 paper strips)

The traditional Jacob's ladder fold can be made either with a long strip of paper folded over at the center or with two strips of paper stapled or pasted together at the ends (diagrams E and F). Strip a is brought straight back in the reverse direction across the top of b, and b is brought straight up across a. This procedure is continued until the two strips are completely interlocked together (diagram G). Two long strips about 1½ inches by 36 inches will form the rosette in diagram H, where the ends of the folded strips have been brought together to make a circle. Such forms can be used as decorations on a tree, on window drapes, and in other ways.

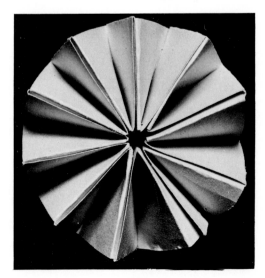

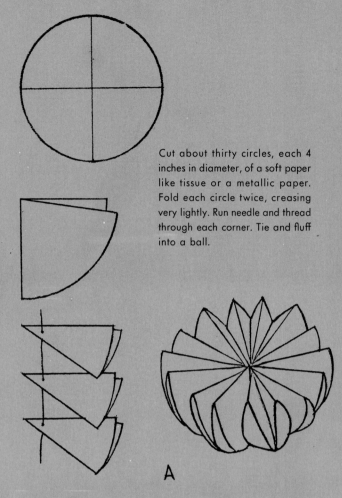

Cut about thirty circles, each 4 inches in diameter, of a soft paper like tissue or a metallic paper. Fold each circle twice, creasing very lightly. Run needle and thread through each corner. Tie and fluff into a ball.

A

These familiar Christmas decorations can be made from lightweight papers like newsprint, butcher paper, or coated metallic paper. For the pleated structure in figure 2, a sheet 18 inches by 24 inches is a good size to use. It is pleated, collapsed flat, stapled in the center, and fanned out with meeting edges fastened together (diagram D). While it is still collapsed, points can be cut off each end and cutouts made in the edges of the folds. The longer the points, the greater will be the expansion qualities of the circle. In diagram C a long strip approximately six or eight times its width is pleated and collapsed, the points are cut off, a hole is punched in the opposite end, and the structure is fanned around into a circular shape. Two ways of making the balls shown on pages 128 and 129 are explained in diagram E. In *a*, ten or twelve circles are creased in the center, stapled or sewed together, spread out, and fastened at alternate edges as shown in *b*. In c and *d* the circles are strung on a thread through the top and bottom to form the ball.

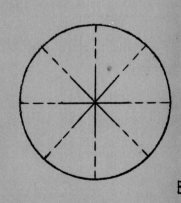

B

Divide a 6-inch circle into eight parts. Cut on dotted lines. Roll each cut section so that a point is formed by the overlapping edges.

Use paste or tape to hold each point. Stack several circles on top of one another and run a needle and thread through the centers.

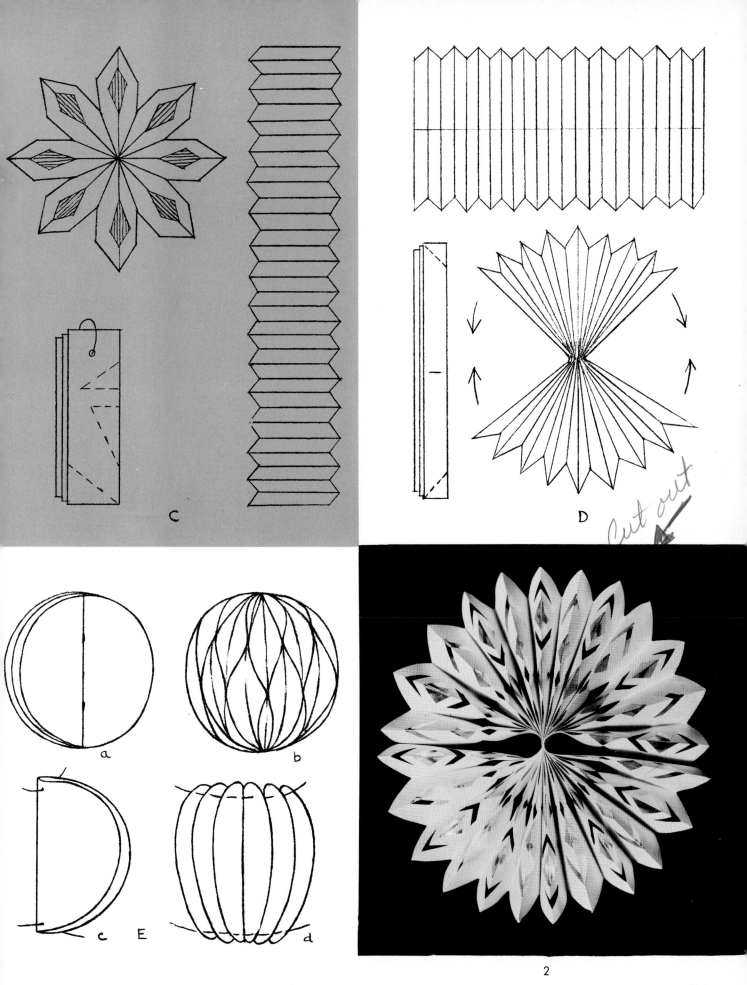

C

D

Cut out

a

b

c   E   d

2

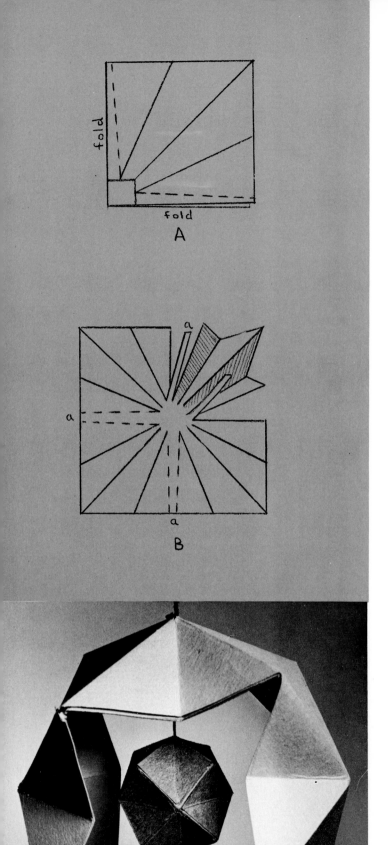

C

The ornament in diagram C is made from two 2½-inch squares of different colored papers. Each square is folded in half twice (diagram A), and a small square is drawn in one corner. The square is then divided into four approximately equal spaces, the slanting dotted line on each side is cut, and the other lines are well creased. When the square is opened up, the lines to the corners are creased so that the fold is on top and the lines on each side are reversed (diagram B). The cut strips (a) are bent outward. One square is placed on top of the other and shifted so that the folded points alternate wih those underneath. The two squares are pasted together in the center. Colored metal foil can be used in place of paper, but it should be tooled rather than creased. For the polyhedron at the left see page 76.

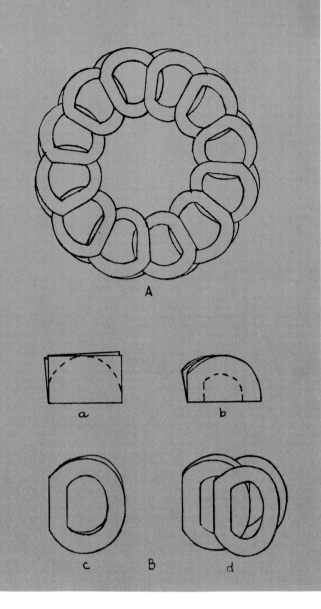

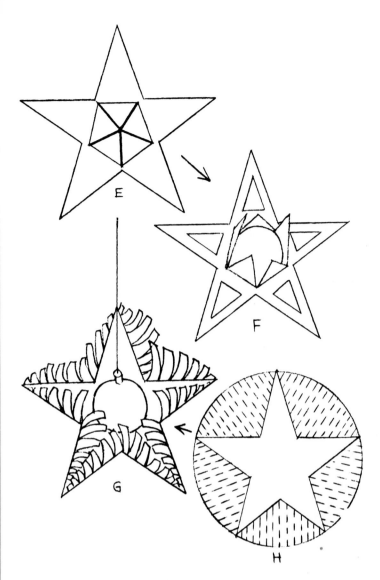

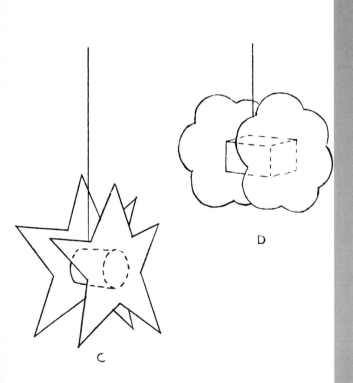

To construct the paper chain in diagram A, a rectangle is folded in half in alternate directions, the corners are rounded off as in *a*, and the center is cut out on the dotted line as in *b*. When opened up, the shape looks like *c*. After several such shapes are cut, they are interlocked one through another as shown in *d*. Another type of ornament, constructed of lightweight cardboard with two identical shapes glued to a small cardboard tube, box, or spool, is shown in diagrams C and D. Paint or sparkle can be added for decoration. In the star ornament of diagrams E and F the heavy lines of the five-sided shape are cut and bent outward and a Christmas tree ball is inserted. The star of diagram G is drawn within a circle and the dotted lines are cut and bent upward.

STARS

PLAN A

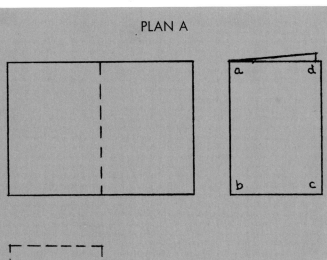

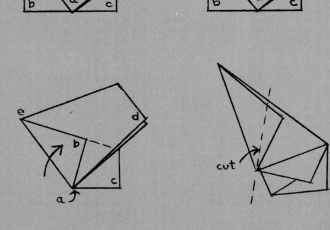

CUTTING A FIVE-POINTED STAR

Plan A. Start with a sheet of typing paper 8½ by 11 inches or any paper of similar proportions. Fold in half. Find center between points *b* and *c*. Bring point *a* to this center. Fold corner *b* over along *ea*. Fold corner *d* under along *eb*. Cut on indicated dotted line.

Plan B. Start with a square and fold it in half from corner to corner. Find the center along side *ad*. Bring point *b* over to this center mark. Fold corner *a* up along *be*. Fold the right half under along *ae*. Turn the shape over and cut on slanting dotted line from one of the lowest points downward.

PLAN B

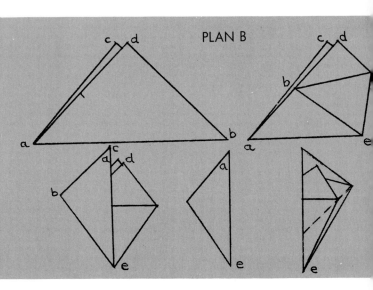

To draw a star, construct a circle with a compass. Draw the diameter and erect a perpendicular. Divide line cb in half at e. Swing an arc from point e, using the radius ed, and find point f. Swing an arc from point d, using df as a radius, and find point g. gd is one-fifth of the outside circle. Use this measurement to divide the circle into five parts. Connect the points and construct a star.

Constructing a five-pointed star.

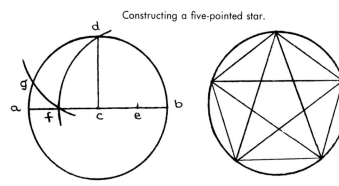

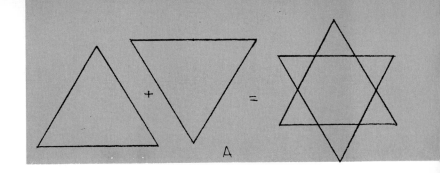

CUTTING A SIX-POINTED STAR

Fold a square in half from corner to corner, then fold in half again. Divide space into thirds. Fold one third upward (*a* over *b*). Fold *c* under. Cut on dotted line. Overlapping two equilateral triangles will also form a six-pointed star. A three-dimensional effect can be achieved by cutting on the dotted line shown in diagram C and lapping point *a* over point *b*. The star can be creased across the points (diagram D) or scored through the points (diagram F). The center can be cut out (diagram E) and a candle inserted. Stars can be used for the top of the Christmas tree, on packages, for mobiles, and for ceiling decorations.

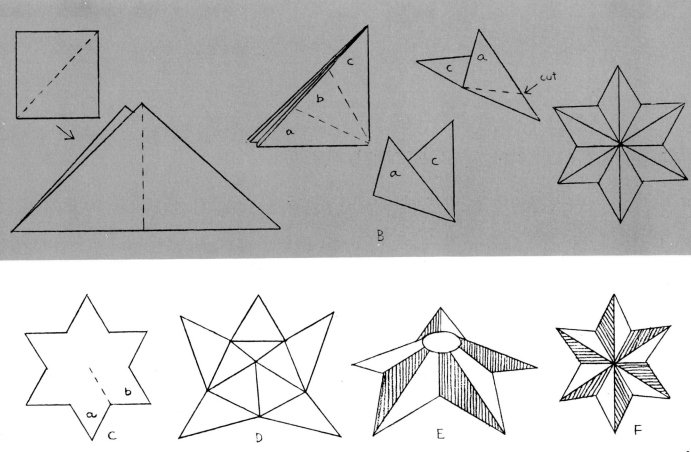

FOUR- AND EIGHT-POINTED STARS

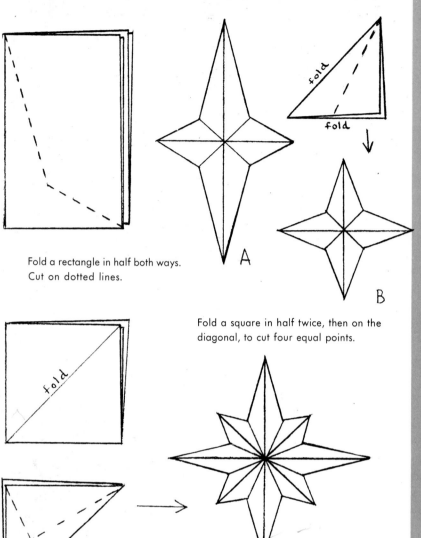

Fold a rectangle in half both ways. Cut on dotted lines.

A

B

Fold a square in half twice, then on the diagonal, to cut four equal points.

C

Fold a square in half both ways, then on the diagonal. Cut on dotted lines.

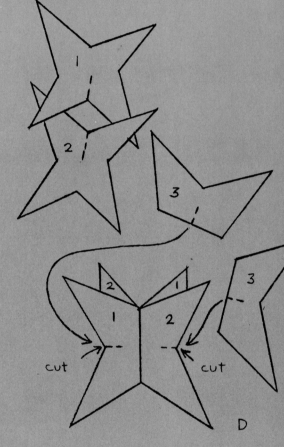

Cut three stars, each with four equal points. Cut on dotted lines of stars 1 and 2 and slip them together. Cut star 3 in half and slit halfway on one edge. Suspend on a string.

cut

cut

D

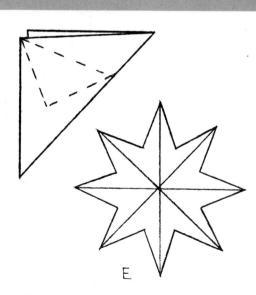

E

To cut eight equal points, fold square twice and then on the diagonal. Cut on dotted lines.

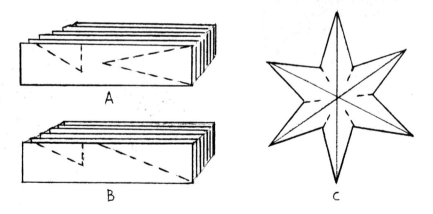

Stars cut from lightweight cardboard and decorated with paint are shown in figures 1, 2, 3, and 4. The structure in figure 5 is made of a lightweight paper, 3 by 11 inches, folded into accordion pleats. Two ways of cutting this form are shown in diagrams A and B. The star in diagram C is scored through each point, and the dotted lines are cut.

1

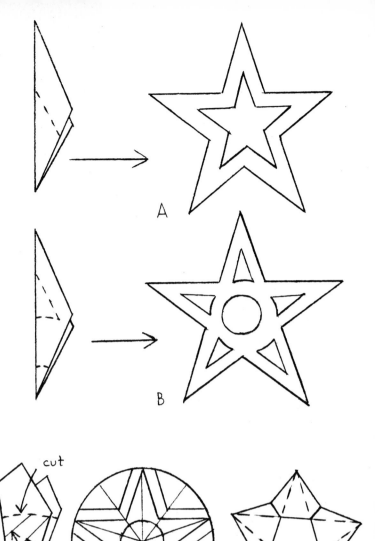

2

A

B

cut

crease

C

D

3

Star snowflakes are traditional yet continually fascinating shapes. Whether they are simple or intricate, the inevitable repetition of the cuts resulting from the folding makes for vitality. The pattern can be drawn first or cut directly in the paper. Diagrams A and B show how shapes can be cut out from folded stars. A star made three-dimensional by scoring is shown in figure 3. Two ways of doing this are explained in diagrams C and D. A square is folded as for a five-pointed star, rounded off at the end, creased, and then opened and creased again.

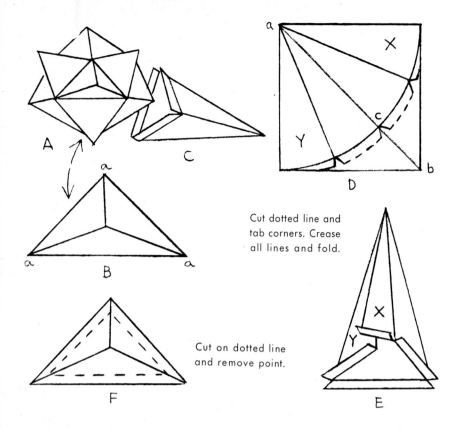

A

B

a

a   a

Cut dotted line and
tab corners. Crease
all lines and fold.

C

a

X

Y

c

b

D

Cut on dotted line
and remove point.

F

X

Y

E

The three-dimensional star on this page is composed of eight projecting three-sided points. It can be suspended as a holiday decoration, and if it is made hollow a light can be inserted inside it.

This star form is built upon the base of an eight-pointed polyhedron ball like the one described on page 76. Over each of the points is slipped a three-sided structure, as shown in diagram C. An arc is drawn in a square and divided into four sections, three of which must be the same width across the base as the base of each side of the polyhedron points (diagram D). Tabs about ¼ inch wide are added at the base of the form. x is lapped over y (diagram E), and the tabs are used to attach the pointed shape to the polyhedron with rubber cement or another adhesive.

To make the star hollow, cut off each point of the polyhedron (diagram F) before attaching the long points. Colored construction papers, or other medium-weight papers like Bristol or tag board, are satisfactory for this structure.

Star-shaped lanterns carried in a procession to herald the Christmas season in Gia Kiem. ➤

BIRDS

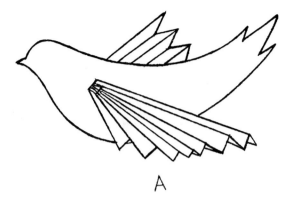

A

Birds, like stars, make festive holiday decorations. When suspended on threads they swing in the air currents in changing moving patterns. The birds shown here are cut from a flat piece of paper, with wings attached on either side. The wings may be pleated, curved, fringed, bent, or rolled, and stapled or pasted to the body shape. The birds on the facing page are folded in half, with the fold coming either on top or at the bottom of the form. The wings and tail can either be cut in one piece with the body or attached separately. Both thin and rather heavy papers can be used for exploring ideas, and it is important to keep in mind that birds should be imaginative and creative rather than naturalistic. Gay colored papers as well as paint, including gold and silver, are effective additions.

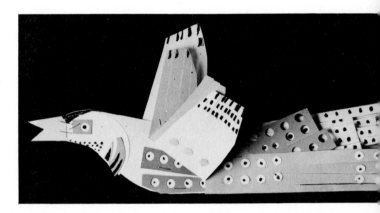

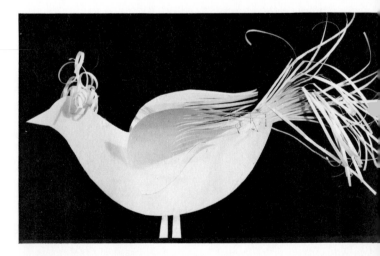

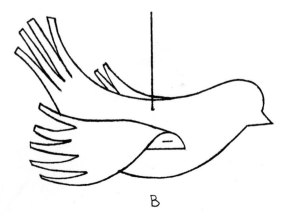

B

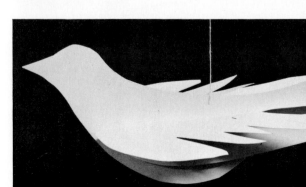

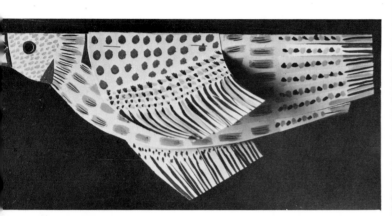

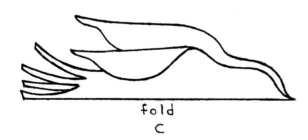

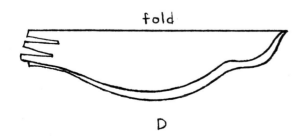

fold

C

fold

D

1

2

The birds on this page are formed of several parts rather than cut from a single piece of paper. They have more detail than the previous examples and rely upon cut areas, scorings, cut paper pieces, and fringe for interest. The examples in figures 2 and 4 are built upon cone shapes. The head of the peacock is attached to the neck with a small brad that serves a double function as an eye. The turkey in figure 1 is structured of lightweight white Bristol with scraps of colored papers added for contrast. In figure 3 the head and body of the owl are cut from one flat piece of paper with the back and front cut identically. The face and breast are superimposed over the front, and the wings are scored and inserted between the front and back pieces.

The birds and the carp on the five pages following are traditional Japanese paper folds based upon the square. In Japan, paper folding is a popular pastime for both children and adults.

3

4

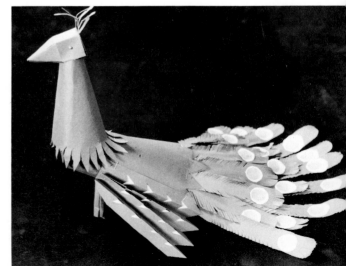

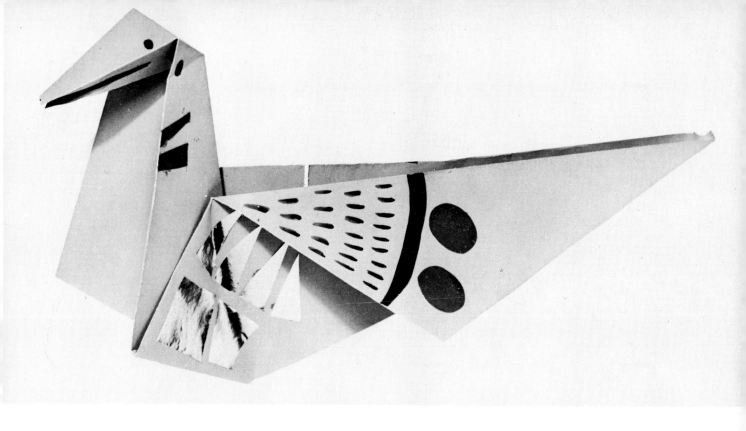

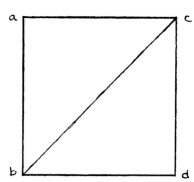

Crease square on diagonal.

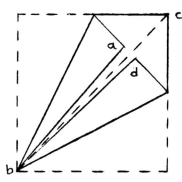

Bring sides *ab* and *bd* to diagonal *bc*.

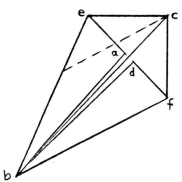

Bring *ec* to *bc*. Fold on dotted line.

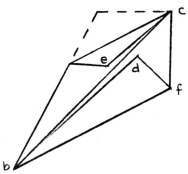

Bring *cf* to *bc* and crease.

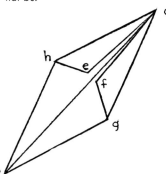

Fold along *bc*.

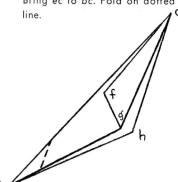

Points *g* and *h* now face downward.

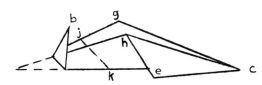

Turn shape upside down. Fold up tip *b* for head. Crease *jk* for neck. Push shape inward to form neck and head.

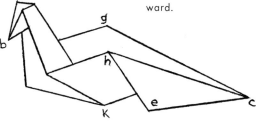

Decorate completed bird with paint or colored papers and suspend on a thread.

147

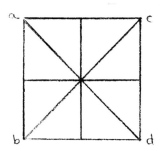
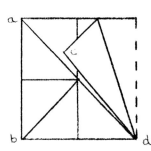
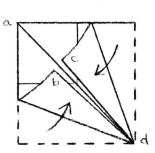
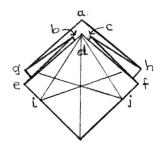

Crease a square on diagonal, vertical, and horizontal lines.

Fold corner c along diagonal ad. Fold corner b along same diagonal, as in making a paper airplane.

Open the folds and note creases radiating from d.

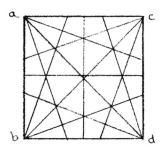
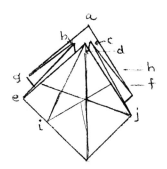
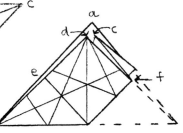
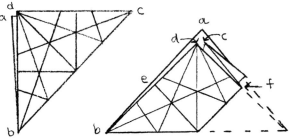

Do the same from a, b, and c. The creases will appear as above.

Fold square on one diagonal.

Grasp point c and push it up and in between points a and d.

Do the same with point b, pushing it in to meet point c.

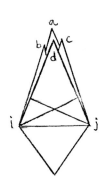
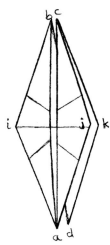
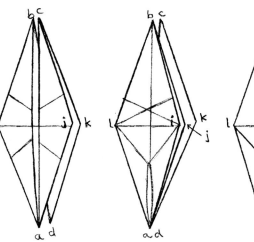

Push point f in along the creased line dj. Push point h in also. Do the same with points e and g along id.

Fold point d down along line ij. Turn over and fold down point a.

Fold point i over onto j. Fold point k back behind l.

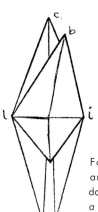
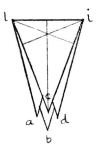

Fold along line li and bring point c down to meet points a and d.

Turn over and fold down point b.

Turn shape upside down. Pull out b and c to form wings. a and d form the head and tail.

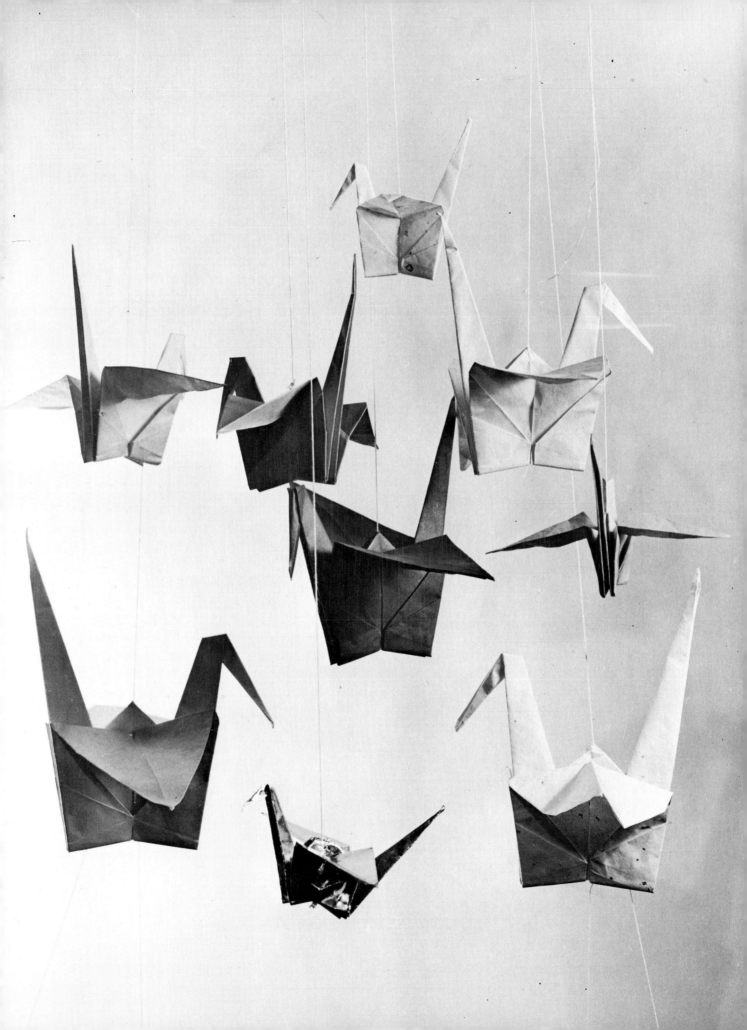

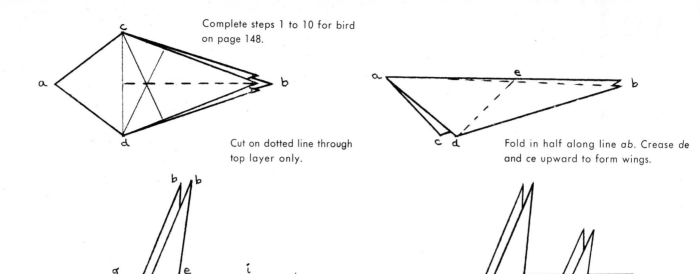

Complete steps 1 to 10 for bird on page 148.

Cut on dotted line through top layer only.

Fold in half along line *ab*. Crease *de* and *ce* upward to form wings.

Fold up tail pieces along *hi*. Crease *fg* to form head.

Push the top fold of the head down and in. Try colored tissue paper.

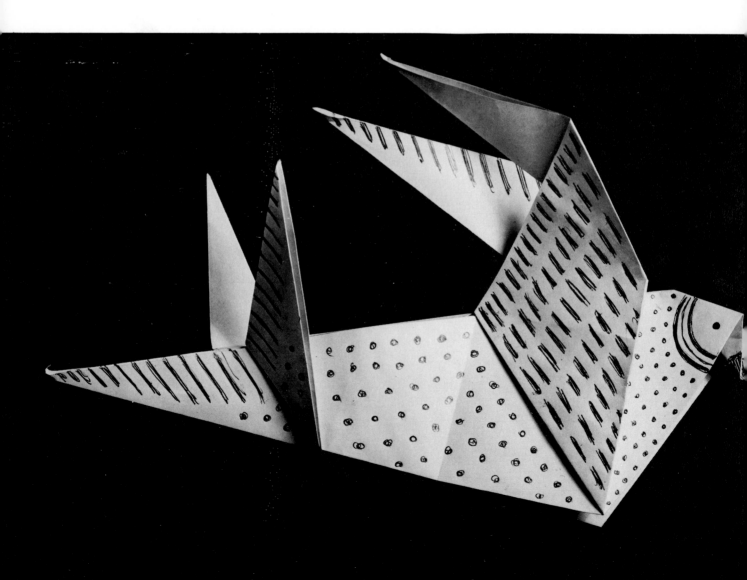

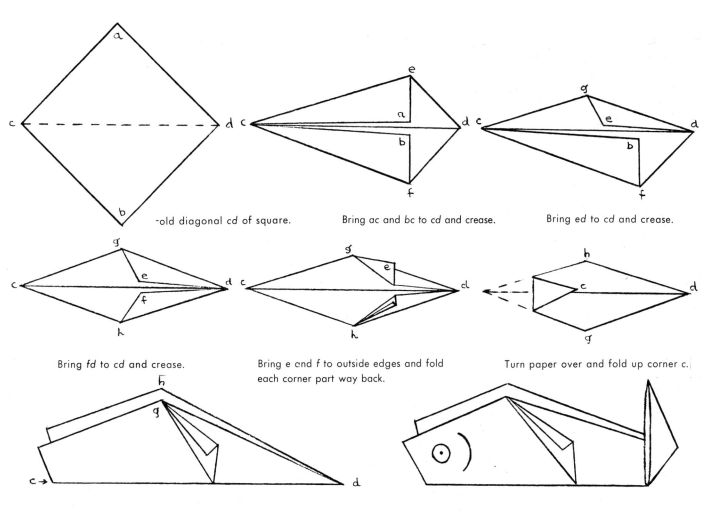

-old diagonal *cd* of square.

Bring *ac* and *bc* to *cd* and crease.

Bring *ed* to *cd* and crease.

Bring *fd* to *cd* and crease.

Bring *e* and *f* to outside edges and fold each corner part way back.

Turn paper over and fold up corner *c*.

Fold up so that point *g* meets point *h*. Crease *cd*.

Fold up tail. Add paint for details.

151

MASKS

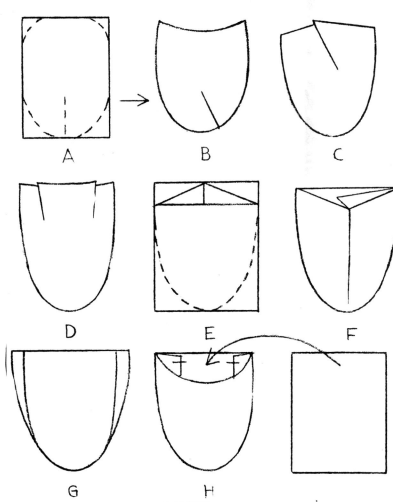

A   B   C

D   E   F

G   H

Bend tabs of G and fasten to flat paper I.

1

2

3

The making of a mask is an opportunity for expression of fantasy and make-believe, calling upon full use of the imagination. It is a wonderful outlet for the creative energies of children, affording much joy and satisfaction. In earlier cultures, masks have often been part of primitive religious observances, as well as an important factor in the theater. Today they are used for Halloween masquerades, parties, parades, creative dramatics, and in other ways. Suggestions for cutting, slitting, and shaping a flat piece of paper to make it rounded are given in the diagrams above. The examples in figures 1, 2, and 3 show how pieces of colored papers can be added for detail to suggest character. On the facing page is seen a mask with attached parts that have been scored, and another made from a cone in which features have been cut.

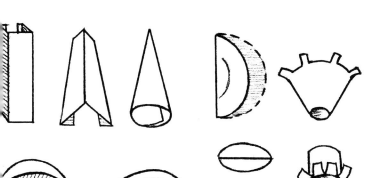

K

SUGGESTIONS FOR FACIAL FEATURES

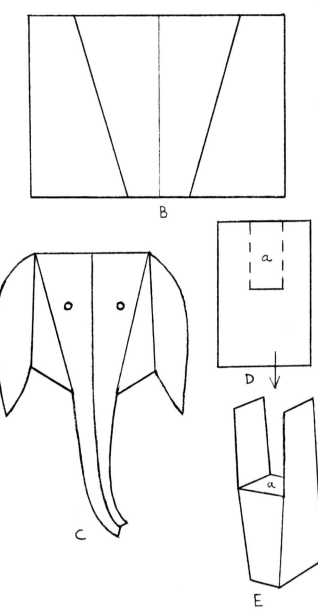

B

C

D

E

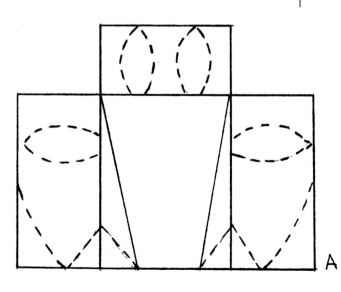

A

The masks on this page are based upon the cube as a basic shape, while those on the facing page are formed of cylinders. Animals are used as examples, but the human face can also be the basis of the design. In making the mask, such identifying factors as the shape and position of the ears, structure of the face, snout, and other parts should be considered. The paper can be fringed, cut, or scored for added character and interest. In figure 1 two boys are shown wearing masks in a parade. On the facing page: teachers in a music workshop.

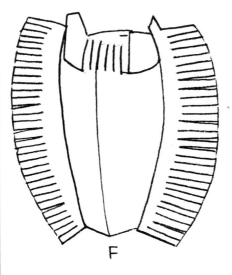

F

3

2

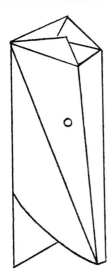

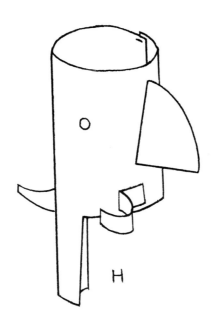

G

H

4

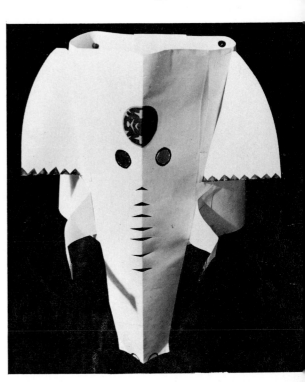

5

VALENTINES

Valentines should be gay and colorful expressions, sentimental within the limits of good taste and design. It is challenging to see in how many ways a shape like the heart can be used for all sorts of delightful structures. Cutouts with charming cupids and hearts made by folding the paper, or hearts formed into containers for holding candy and flowers are suggested here. Gay banners, streamers, and flags are very festive when suspended in the air. Valentines would not be complete without the traditional box elegantly covered with bows of crepe paper and ribbon streamers.

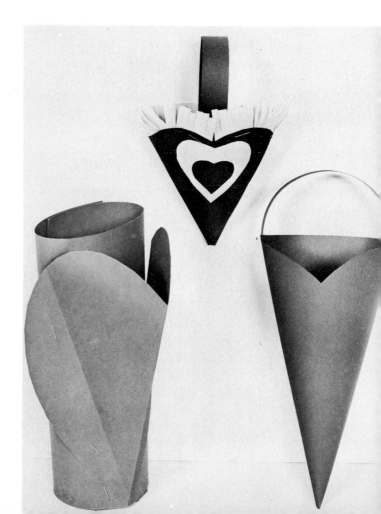

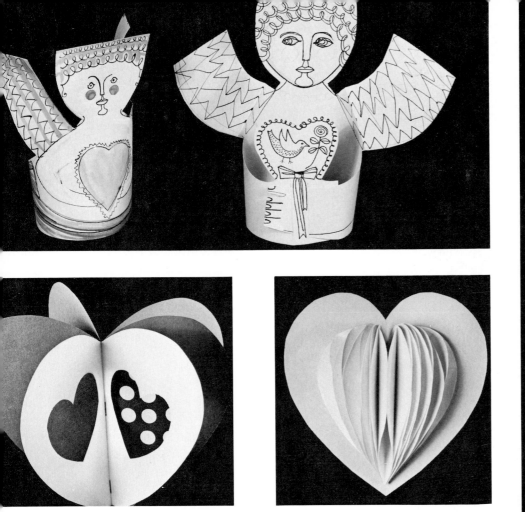

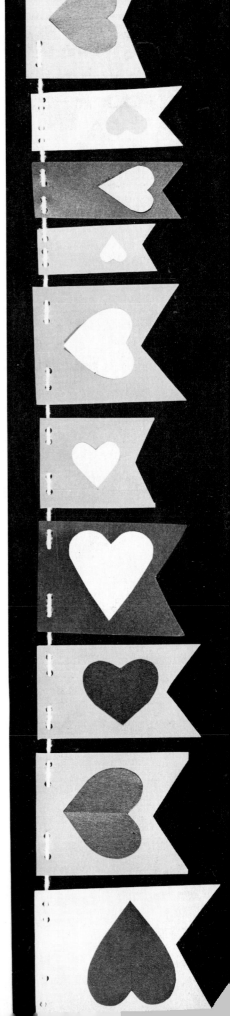

EASTER FORMS

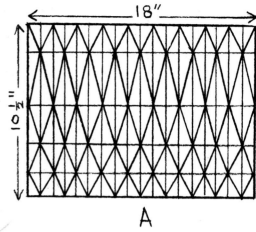

A

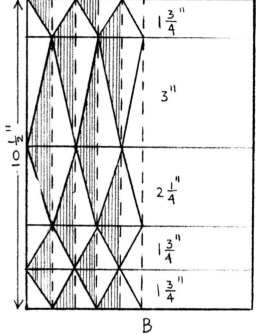

B

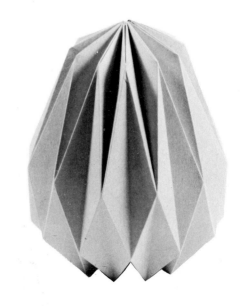

Easter is portrayed here by the symbols of spring. Rabbits are shown assembled from cones, as above, or cut and folded from a single piece of paper, as in the photograph on the facing page. Various ways of making eggs are also suggested. The example at the right, made from a rectangle of colored construction paper, is explained in the diagrams above as well as in the section on scoring on page 56. More rabbits will be found on page 163.

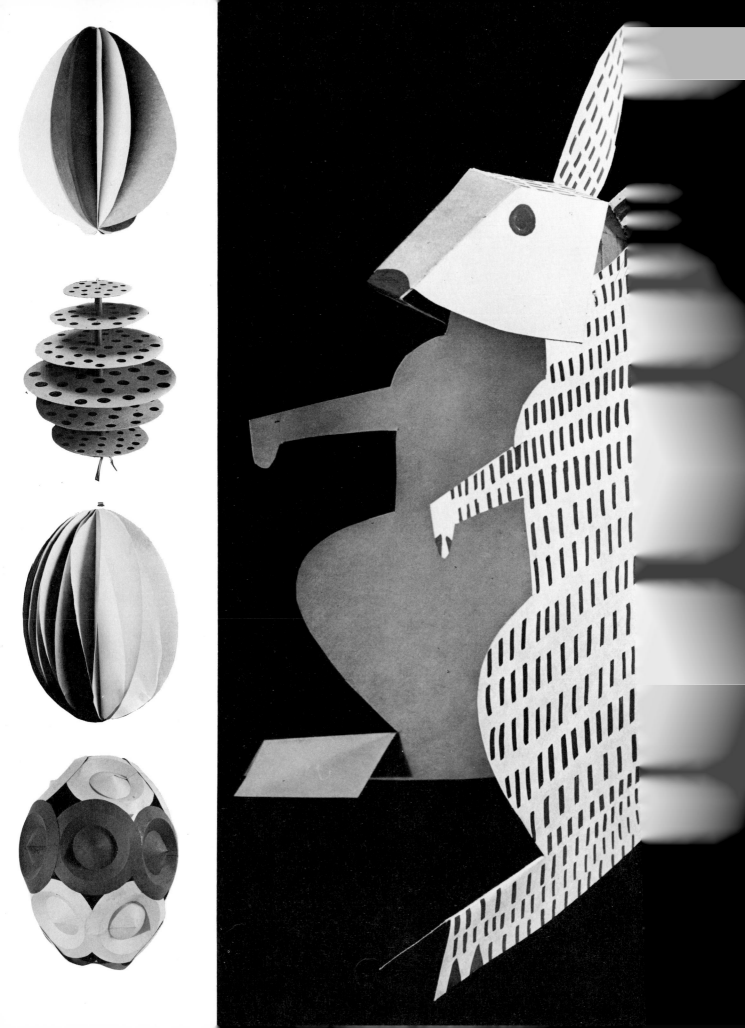

See diagrams at right for woven basket. Fold rectangle in half and cut into pieces *a* and *b*. Fold *a* and *b* in half and cut strips in each from the fold edge on the dotted lines. Those in *a* should be the same length as the width of the paper; those in *b* about ¼ inch longer. Weave a strip at a time, starting at fold edges. Put first strip of *a* through inside strip of *b*. Then let second strip of *b* go through first strip of *a*. Keep weaving all the way across. Push this strip down and start second strip of *a*. Continue until all are woven.

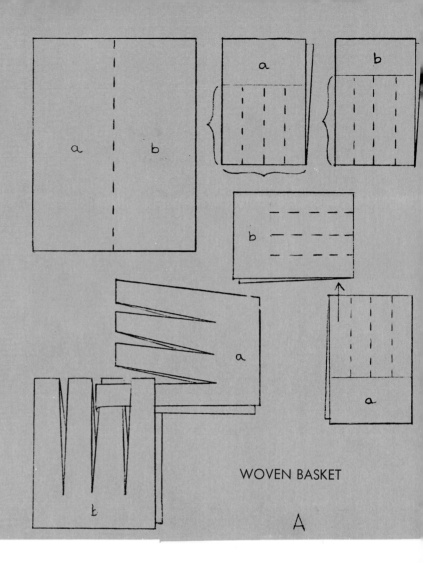

WOVEN BASKET

A

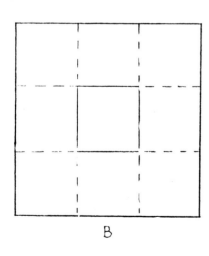

B

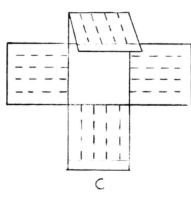

C

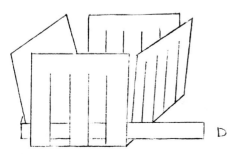

D

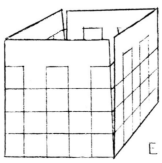

E

An Easter basket can be made by weaving together strips of colored papers. A square is folded into nine equal parts, and the corners are cut out (diagram B). Then ½-inch strips are cut, starting about ½ inch from the edge of each side. The strips can be slit with a sharp knife, or the paper can be folded and cut in from the fold edge, as shown in diagram C. The four sides are bent upward, and ½-inch strips are woven around the box. If the second strip is begun at a different corner from the first, it will help hold the basket in shape. An example of a woven basket is shown on page 97. Other suggestions for baskets are given in the section under May Day.

The basket above is formed of a sheet of newsprint to which woven strips of poster paper have been pasted. A square is creased to form sixteen squares. Lines *ab, cd, ef,* and *gh* are creased. The paper is turned over, and *ac, bd, eg, fh, ij, kl, jl,* and *ik* are creased. The paper is turned back over. The section *mnop* is the base. The corners marked X are folded under. *ik* and *jl* are folded under, forming two sides of the basket. *im, jn, ko,* and *lp* are pinched outward and folded back behind the shaded portions of the square, and the top of the flap is bent down on the other two sides.

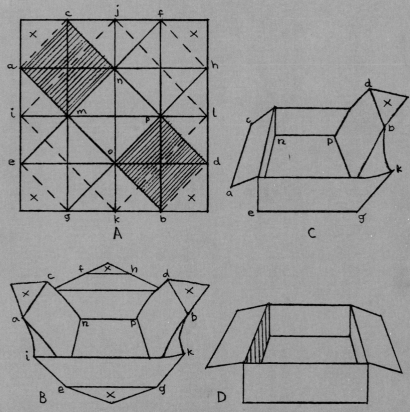

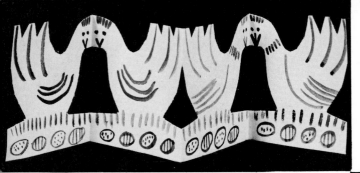

Here we have a number of variations on the same subject, including the multiple-fold cut of the repeated shapes of the chickens at the left, and the box structure composed of sections of Bristol board taped together.

The delightful creations above and below are cut out of butcher paper and stapled together. Watercolor brush strokes add surface interest. The cylindrical structure at the left is formed of colored construction papers.

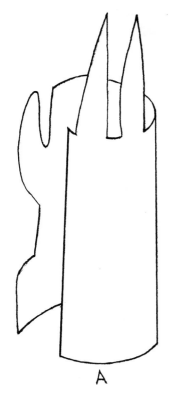

A

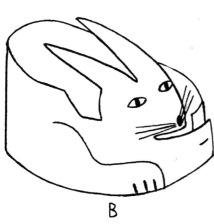

B

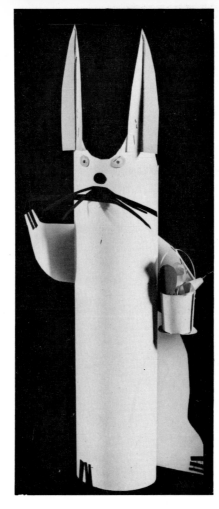

Rabbits constructed from a single sheet of paper shaped into a cylindrical form can be beautiful in their restraint and simplicity. In these examples lines and spots have been added as design elements. The structure below was cut, shaped, and stapled to create the desired form.

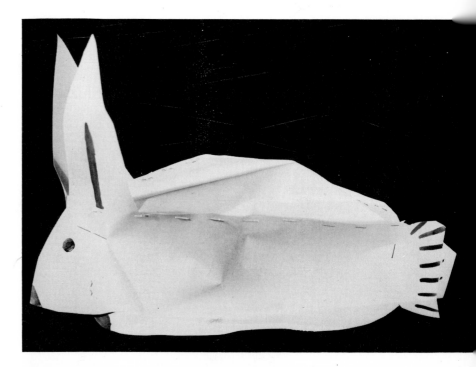

MAY DAY BASKETS

The ancient festival of May Day has been observed in numerous parts of the world as far back as the time of the Romans, when the occasion was celebrated with beautiful floral games. During the Middle Ages it was the custom to bring home flowers on the first day of May, and in medieval and Tudor England May Day was a great public holiday when people went "a-Maying." Processions carrying branches of trees and flowers marched triumphantly into towns and villages, culminating with festivities about the Maypole. With its gay and colorful ribbon or paper streamers held by intertwining dancers weaving in and out around the central staff, the Maypole was an important part of the glorious pageantry associated with the crowning of the May queen.

Childhood memories will be brought to mind by the wonderful custom of giving May baskets, which, filled with fresh spring blossoms and hung from the doorknob or placed upon the doorstep, were a source of surprise and delight. A number of ways of making baskets, some of them familiar and traditional, will be found in this section. Simple, yet fascinating, structures like these become personal expressions when pleasing color combinations and interesting materials are used, and decorative elements like fringe, bows, cut paper shapes, and paint are added. The baskets illustrated at the bottom of this page and the next are made of colored construction and tissue papers, enhanced with cutout paper pieces combined with brush strokes. The example in figure 7 is constructed like the folded polyhedron on page 76.

1

2

3

4

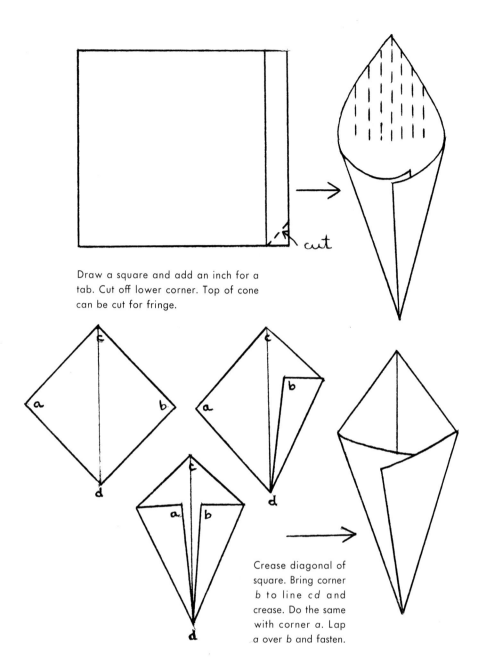

Draw a square and add an inch for a tab. Cut off lower corner. Top of cone can be cut for fringe.

Crease diagonal of square. Bring corner *b* to line *cd* and crease. Do the same with corner *a*. Lap *a* over *b* and fasten.

5   6   7

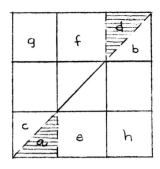

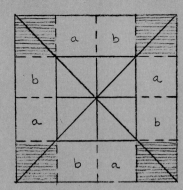

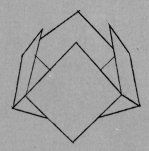

Divide square into thirds both ways and crease lines. Crease one diagonal. Cut out triangles *a* and *d*. Fold basket, fastening triangles *b* and *c* as laps under *e* and *f*. Corners *g* and *h* can be folded outward.

Fold lines. Cut on dotted lines. Lap *a* over *b* and fasten.

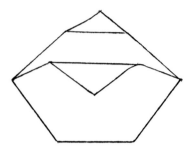

Divide a square into thirds both ways. Round the corners and cut them off. Cut out sections *e*, *f*, *g*, *h* on dotted lines. Use *a*, *b*, *c*, *d* for flaps.

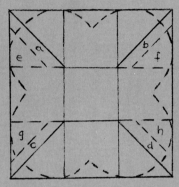

Fold corners and cut out a design.

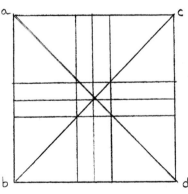

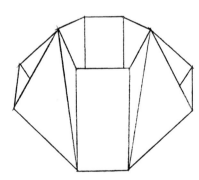

Crease vertical and horizontal lines. Turn paper over and crease diagonals. Bring corners *a* and *b* together and fasten. Do the same with corners *c* and *d*. Try different arrangements for variations on this basket.

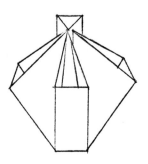

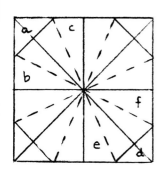

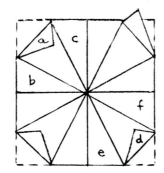

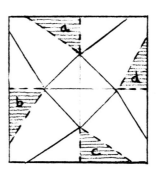

Cut a square in half diagonally. Divide into four equal parts and fold on dotted lines. Fasten with a tie through holes in the outer corners.

Fold a square in half in both directions. Fold both diagonals. Divide spaces between in half, as indicated by dotted lines. The paper should be turned over so that these can be creased on the opposite side. Fold *b* and *c* to meet under flap *a*; *e* and *f* to meet under flap *d*. Fasten.

Cut out triangles *a, b, c, d*; use other triangles for overlaps.

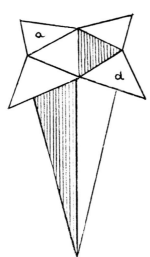

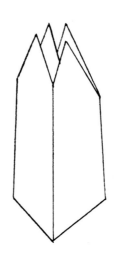

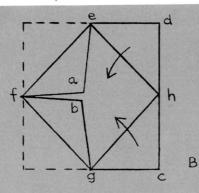

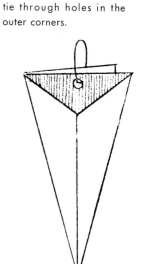

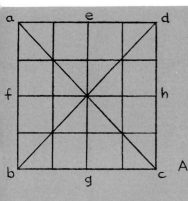

A

B

Crease all lines in A well. Fold each corner to center as in B. Turn B over and fold corners to center as in C. Turn C back over. Pull up each corner and pop up the center, emphasizing all creases. Put one finger into each corner opening and squeeze fingers together.

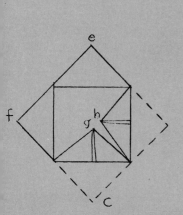

C

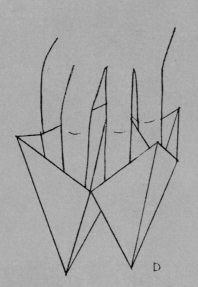

D

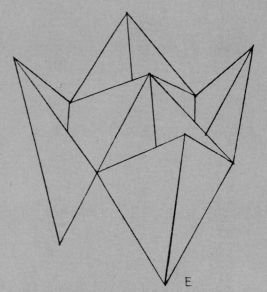

E

167

The square has been used as the basis for the basket designs on the previous pages. On this page and the next, the circle and rectangle are employed. These forms can be varied in many ways by combining different kinds of papers and colors as well as various decorative items. Fringe, cutout areas, and paint and crayon are all suggested for use.

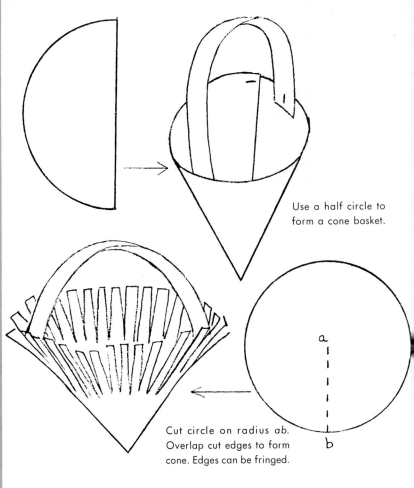

Use a half circle to form a cone basket.

Cut circle on radius *ab*. Overlap cut edges to form cone. Edges can be fringed.

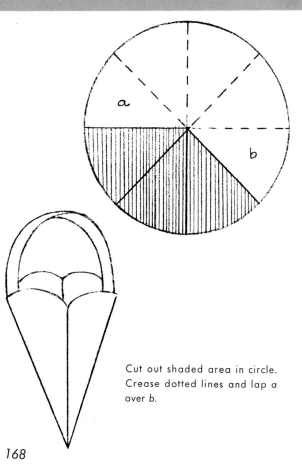

Cut out shaded area in circle. Crease dotted lines and lap *a* over *b*.

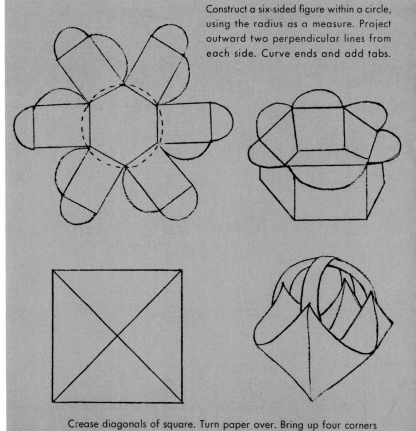

Construct a six-sided figure within a circle, using the radius as a measure. Project outward two perpendicular lines from each side. Curve ends and add tabs.

Crease diagonals of square. Turn paper over. Bring up four corners and hold together with handles.

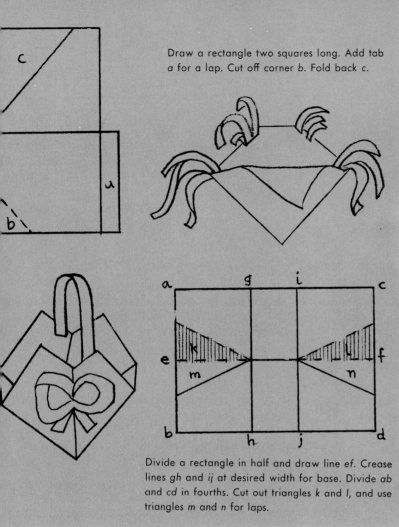

Draw a rectangle two squares long. Add tab a for a lap. Cut off corner b. Fold back c.

Fold all four edges of a rectangle the same width. Cut dotted lines and fold. Use corners a, b, c, d for overlaps.

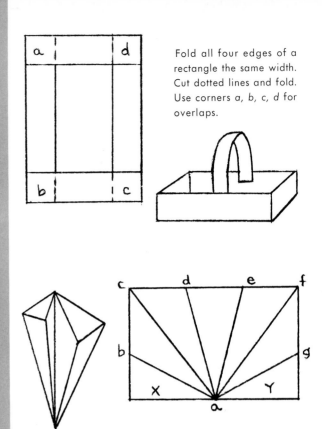

Divide a rectangle in half and draw line ef. Crease lines gh and ij at desired width for base. Divide ab and cd in fourths. Cut out triangles k and l, and use triangles m and n for laps.

Fold rectangle from center point a of one side to opposite corners c and f. Divide into equal spaces. Fold ab upward, ac downward, ad and ae upward, af downward, and ag upward. Overlap triangles x and y.

Divide a rectangle into six squares. Fold lines ab, cd, and ef. Cut off rounded corners. Cut lines eg and fh. Fold top and bottom corners on left and cut out c stencil design. Use flaps x and y for overlaps.

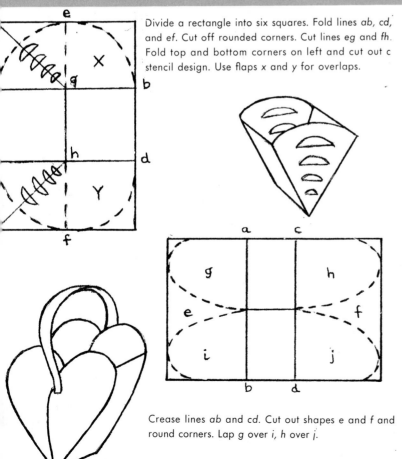

Crease lines ab and cd. Cut out shapes e and f and round corners. Lap g over i, h over j.

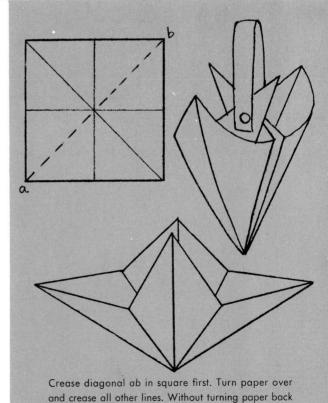

Crease diagonal ab in square first. Turn paper over and crease all other lines. Without turning paper back over, lift corners a and b and bring them together. Lap a over b and fasten.

169

GIFT CARDS

Gift and greeting cards can be distinctive and beautiful in design. A number of ways in which they can be folded flat, but become three-dimensional when opened, are presented here. In diagram A, stiff paper is scored so as to bend and fold flat. The centers of each section except the back one are removed, and various shapes are fastened in the openings. In some cards, slits are used so that shapes can interlock. The example in figure 6 shows a folded sheet with a cutout opening related to the painted design within. Further possibilities are shown in the diagrams, which are based upon techniques described in other parts of the book.

1

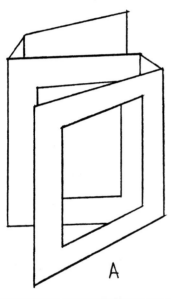

A

2

3

4

5

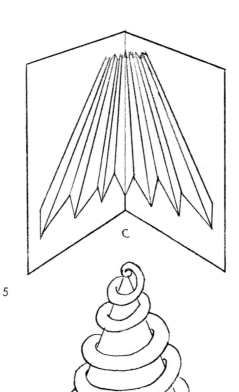

C

8

6

D

E

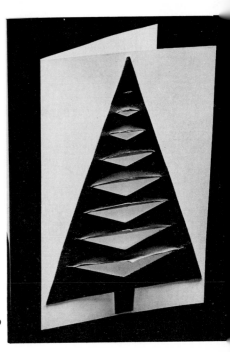

9

Crease squares in center
and staple together.

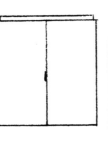

B

7

10

ENVELOPES AND WRAPPINGS

Envelopes can be constructed to hold cards or flat gifts. The card is laid on a sheet of paper and traced, with about ⅛ inch extra allowed all around. Flaps are added for folding. Envelopes can be made of colored construction papers, Kraft paper, tag board, and similar materials. A repeat design can be applied directly to the folder for decoration or to tissue paper, which is then inserted for an attractive liner (diagram C). Block prints and stencils can be used for making such designs. The wrappings in figure 1 are decorated with potato prints, block prints, and cut papers.

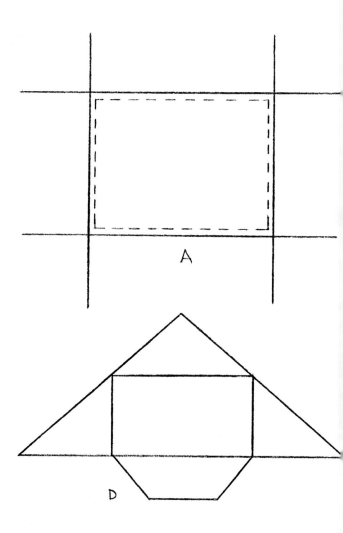

A

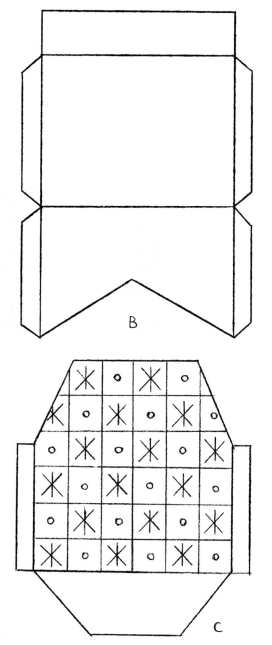

B

D

C

1

The wrapping of a package can be an esthetic experience if it is thought of in terms of design and color. With a little imagination, exciting results can be achieved by employing such decorative elements as fringe, printed designs, and cut papers. The print in figure 2 was made from an art gum eraser. The example in figure 3 is wrapped with two colors of crepe paper.

2

1

MAKING A BOX

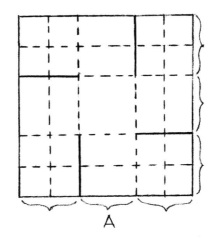

A

Start with a square, for example one 9 by 9 inches or 12 by 12 inches. Divide into thirds vertically and horizontally to make nine squares. Crease well. Fold each strip around the central square in half. Cut on heavy lines.

Fold strips again on outer dotted lines, as in diagram B. Fold on second dotted lines to form sides of box.

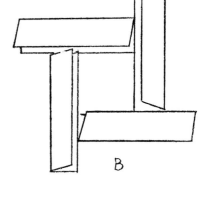

B

Flap a slips under side b. Do the same at all corners. This forms the box without using paste or staples. Make lid with narrower sides. Decorate with paper, paint, or crayon.

3

C

173

PARTY DECORATIONS

Planning and carrying out decorations for parties, banquets, and other events can be an exciting adventure when approached in the spirit of exploration with the pleasure of the occasion kept in mind. The decorative scheme should be conceived in terms of design, the aim being to achieve harmonious relationships and unification of all the parts. The problem of what to do and where to begin is one that causes confusion for many people who feel totally inadequate and lacking in ideas of how to proceed with a decorating plan. Working together in a group where enthusiasms and concepts can be shared with others sometimes provides the necessary stimulus to the imagination. Referring to different parts of this book for inspiration will help to focus attention on shapes appropriate in character for various needs. Some of the beautiful abstract forms in the front section should be considered as possible source material. The section on holidays indicates directions that might be pursued for further development. In this part will be found stars, angels, birds, and other items especially suitable as decorative structures that can be repeated and varied to fit the desired plan.

The kind of festivity and the age of the participants help to determine the character of the decorations and provide a starting point for action. Recourse to stereotyped forms or preconceived static plans can be avoided with a little imagination and willingness to adventure with new ideas. There is no limit to the possibilities that can be evolved if some of the directions suggested are explored.

The approach to the problem is an esthetic one, involving visual harmonies of colors, shapes, forms, lines, movement, and decorative detail. The size of the room to be decorated must be considered. If it is a large one, the decorative elements must be conceived on a large scale in order to carry impact and make the desired impression. The structural elements, such as walls, windows, doors, posts, floor area, ceiling, and mantel, as well as separate parts like tables and light fixtures, should be noted as possible space to be incorporated into the total decorative effect.

The decorative elements employed may be either flat or three-dimensional, depending upon the areas in which they are to be used—against a wall or ceiling, suspended to hang from above, arranged on a table or mantel, or elsewhere. The parts can then be related by repetition of some of the shapes and colors, working for a rhythmic pattern.

The nature of the decorations will help to determine the types of papers selected for use. The paper can be delicate, sturdy, colorful, shiny, or have whatever quality is needed. Colored construction and metallic coated papers are suitable and attractive for many occasions. Crepe paper can be used in new and different ways. Tissue paper is effective when strength is not needed. Cellophane is colorful and delicate and can be effectively related to heavier structures, as in the Madonna window on page 31. When large size papers are needed it is well to investigate available supplies; however, wrapping papers that come by the yard or roll are generally satisfactory.

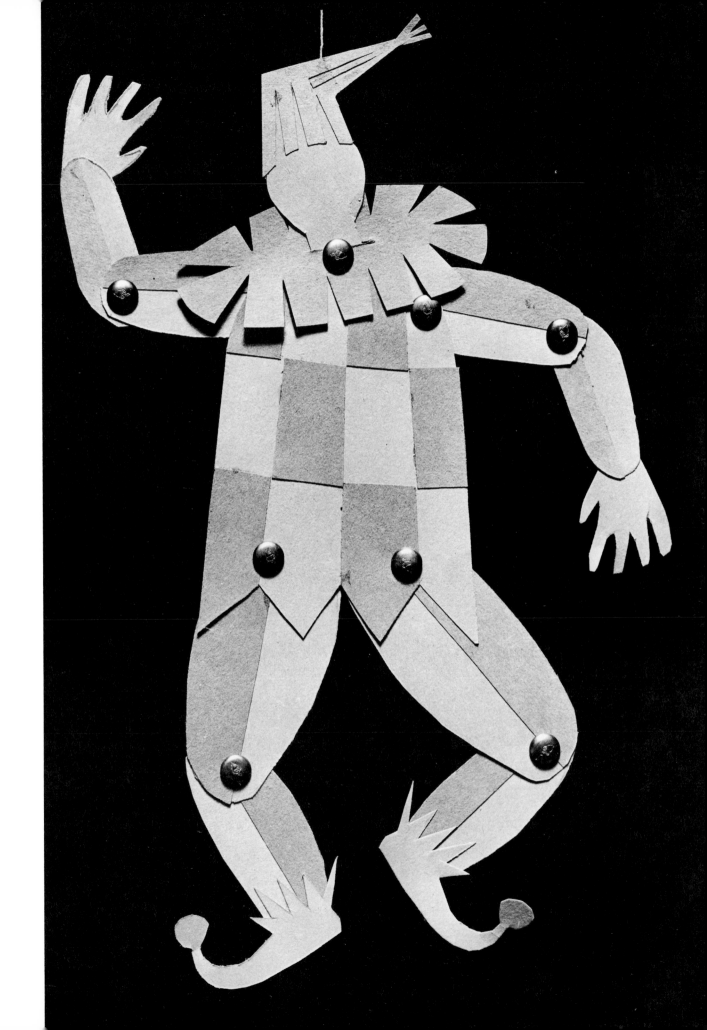

1

2

3

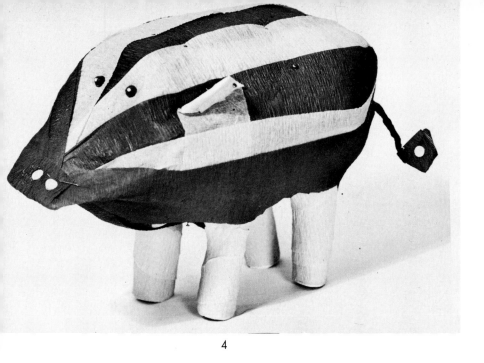

4

5

Parties suggest fun and excitement, whether they are for children or for adults. A stimulating setting for such events can be created through pleasing table arrangements, which provide many opportunities for designing and constructing decorations of paper. Centerpieces can be gay and imaginative like the old witch, who might be accompanied by paper cats with fringed whiskers and tails, or the Uncle Sam created by a child for a luncheon, suggesting a patriotic theme. The decorative pig above has a stuffed paper sack body covered with colorful crepe paper strips held together with pins and a little rubber cement. This is a simple but effective way to create modeled forms. The bright carousel forms the centerpiece for the party on the facing page. Place cards, nut cups, and favors to add to the total effect will be found on the pages following.

6

7

177

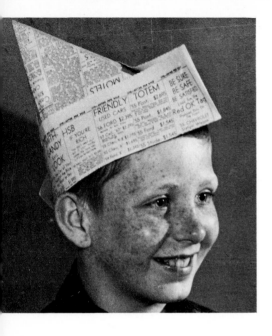

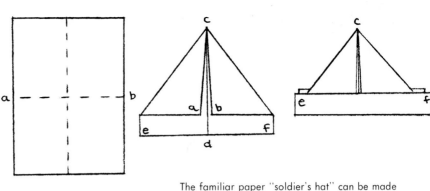

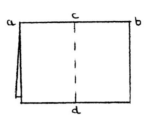

The familiar paper "soldier's hat" can be made of a piece of newspaper approximately 16 by 20 inches in size, creased in the center in both directions. After it is folded in half, the two upper corners are brought over to the center line and the bottom is folded up at the front and back.

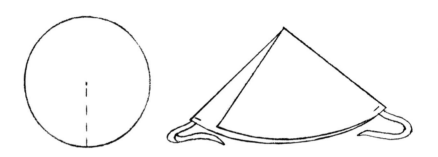

An attractive garden or beach hat can be made from a cone by cutting a circle about 15 inches in diameter out of a stiff paper like tag board. The cone is shaped to head size, and strong ties like cotton roving yarn are attached to the sides. The hat can be decorated with crayon or paint. Cheesecloth glued to the tag board before it is cut adds strength, and a coat of shellac provides greater permanence.

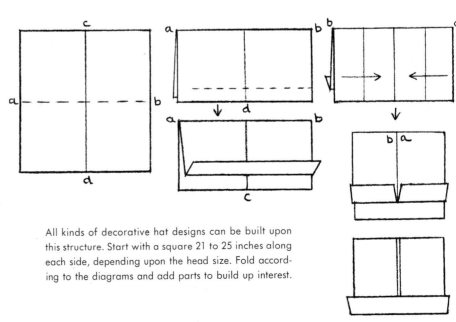

All kinds of decorative hat designs can be built upon this structure. Start with a square 21 to 25 inches along each side, depending upon the head size. Fold according to the diagrams and add parts to build up interest.

178

Paper hats are a part of childhood experience, whether made of newspaper for play and make-believe or of crepe paper, decorated with colorful streamers. Adults, too, find opportunities for using gaily decorative hats on such occasions as New Year's Eve and Halloween. Cones and cylinders, as well as many other approaches, can be used as starting points in constructing a hat. The examples on this page are made of crepe paper, but construction papers, colored tissues, and other varieties should also be considered.

1

2

3

4

5

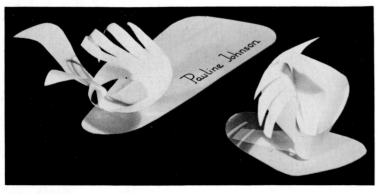

7

PLACE CARDS AND FAVORS

A personal quality is added to the party table with place cards. The plans suggested here should assist in developing ideas. Some are folded at the base (figure 1); others on top, or at the sides. In figure 3 the bird is cut from the half that folds back. This card is all one piece and, like the others near it, is decorated with cut paper pieces. In figures 6 and 7 the shapes are attached to the name card with paste or staples. Other possibilities are the napkin holders at the bottom of the page, which can also be used as place cards and favors.

6

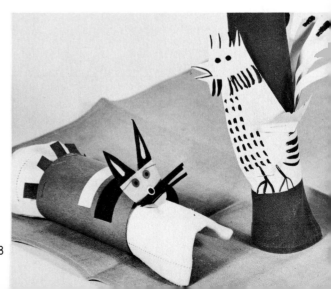

8

1

2

3

Some of these suggestions for party favors are cut from folded sheets of paper, as described elsewhere in the book. The intriguing bird is made of paper rolled into a cylinder and glamorized with sparkle and paint. The Thanksgiving favor in figure 1 was designed by a child, who slit two identical shapes and fitted them together. The paper cup is given character by the rabbit's head, which has been slit on each side and inserted over the edge.

4

5

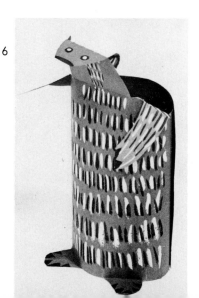

6

7

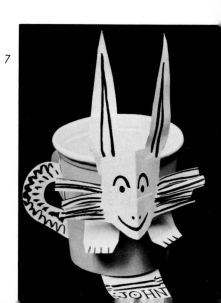

NUT CUPS

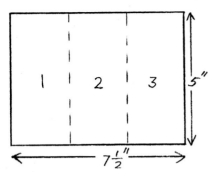

Fold on dotted lines.

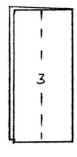

Fold on dotted line.

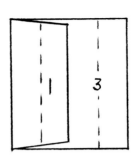

Open up 3. 2 is
under 1.

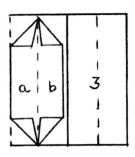

Fold two top corners of 1
to dotted line. Do same
with bottom corners. Fold
b over onto a.

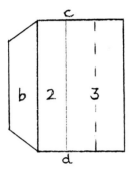

Fold on line cd so that 3
covers 2 and b.

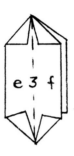

1 and 2 are under 3.

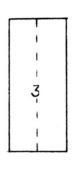

Fold corners of 3
to dotted line. Fold
e over onto f.

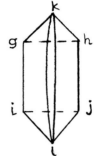

Fold on lines gh
and ij.

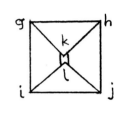

Points k and l will
meet at center.

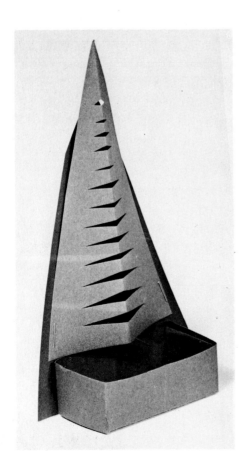

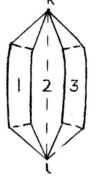

Open up k and l. Lift 1
and 3 and form a box.

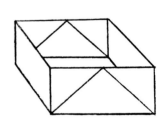

Crease edges and corners well.
Box can be used for nuts, candy,
or pins.

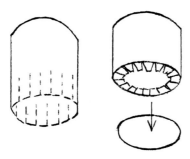

Make a cylinder shape. Slit edges around one end and fold inward. Cut a circle to fit the base and paste to the slits.

1

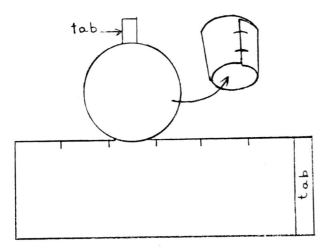

Draw a rectangle and divide into six equal spaces, each 1 inch wide, plus a tab at one end. Draw an attached circle 2 inches in diameter with a tab on the opposite edge. Cut out, making certain the circle is firmly attached to the rectangle. Form a cylinder and paste or staple the tab. Fit the circle into the opening and paste the small tab.

2

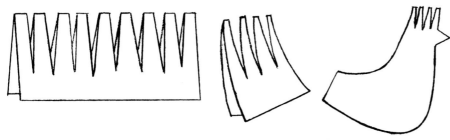

The cup in figure 3 is designed with several thin colored papers, most of which have been cut double with the fold edge on top. Two rows of notched paper form the structure of the cup, and the body of the chicken is attached to the inner row. Notched papers form wings and tail and are fastened to the flat body shape.

3

1

2

3

4

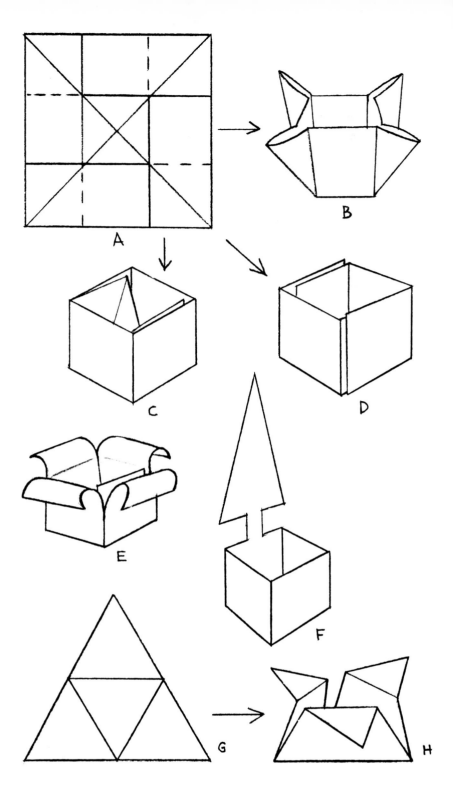

There are infinite possibilities for variety and individuality in the designing of nut cups, even when they are based upon the same general shape. For instance, the square at the top can be folded into a box without cutting (diagrams B and C) or cut on the dotted lines and folded as in diagram D. To vary the edges, parts can be extended on one or more sides. A form made with a triangular base and an extended triangle on each side is shown in figure 3.

The nut cups on this page are examples of a variety of types, which are presented as suggestions for the development of additional ideas. The examples in figures 1 and 2 are both made from the plans in diagrams A and B. In figure 2 a name card is combined with the cup. The clown is cut from a folded paper with the fold at the top. At the base it is spread out and straddles the cup to which it is fastened by the feet. The hands are held together with staples, and a ruff circles the neck. The two bird-shaped cups, explained in diagrams C and D, are made more interesting by the addition of painted detail.

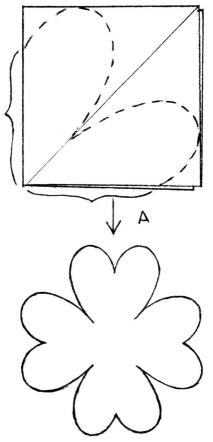

A

B

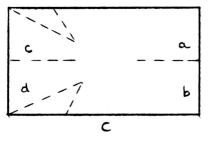

C

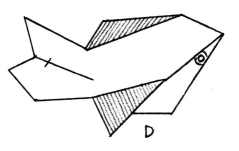

D

1

2

3

4

COSTUMES

Many opportunities for making costumes of paper are provided by parties, plays, and pageants. Sometimes only a suggestion—a collar, a hat, or a jerkin—is needed to convey an idea. More emphasis is then placed upon the use of the imagination, with reliance upon gesture and other forms of expression. Costumes of butcher paper like those in figure 1 can be decorated with paint or cut paper to represent specific characters. Children should be encouraged to use materials creatively.

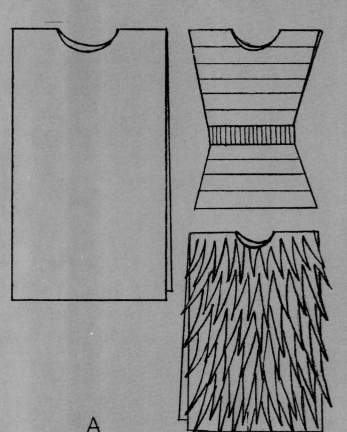

A

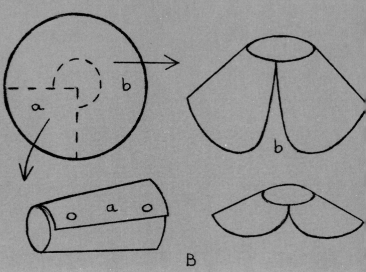

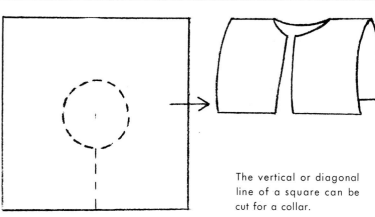

B

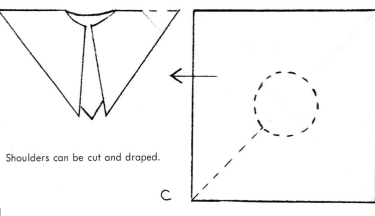

The vertical or diagonal line of a square can be cut for a collar.

Shoulders can be cut and draped.

C

1

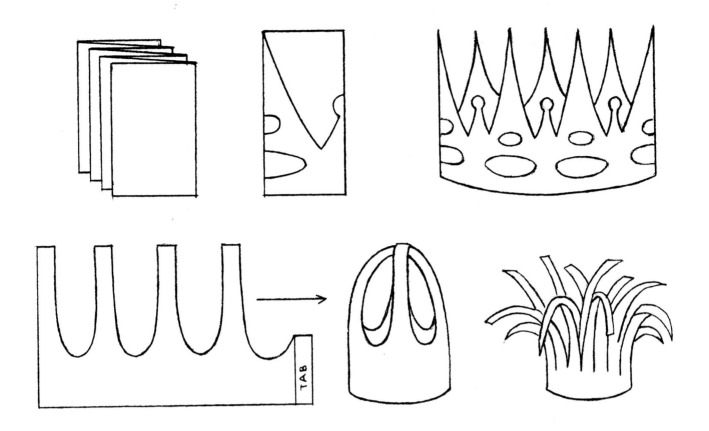

CROWNS   **HELMETS**   **HISTORICAL HEADGEAR**

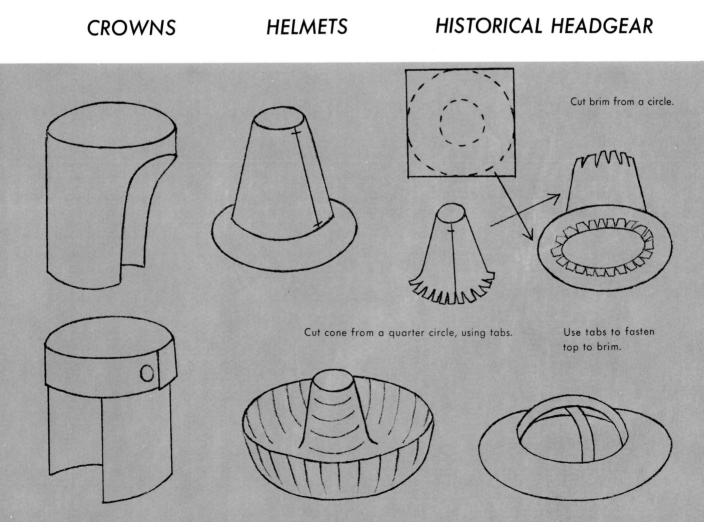

Cut brim from a circle.

Cut cone from a quarter circle, using tabs.

Use tabs to fasten top to brim.

A

TREES

Trees vary from diminutive table models to large-scale structures used for backgrounds in staging or display. They can be formed of cardboard, tissue paper, old newspapers, or other papers, and there are wide possibilities for variations in design. Cutting, curling, fringing, scoring, and other approaches for working with paper, described on previous pages, make it possible to develop ideas appropriate for the specific purpose.

The tree in diagram A can be constructed from large cardboard boxes used for packing mattresses and furniture, or from heavier material like beaver board. Structures like this must be supported from the back unless they are used against a wall. Leaves can be painted, fringed, or scored down the center and slit at one end for a sculptural effect.

The examples at the bottom of this page and the next show small branches or twigs to which have been fastened colored tissue paper flowers and leaves. They are held upright on a table by chunks of clay. The bare twigs can be painted with enamel colors. Special trees for Valentine's Day, Easter, or Christmas make attractive interest centers for table decorations.

The tree at the right, of traditional European origin, is simple and fun to make. Newspapers are spread out on the floor or table, overlapped at the edges, and rolled together. One after another is inserted as they are rolled into a cylinder (diagram B). The height of the tree depends upon the number of papers used. The cylinder is cut with a butcher knife or other sharp knife into long slits (diagram C). One hand is inserted down into the slit end of the cylinder, and the center part is gradually pulled out and shaken briskly from time to time, until a long stalk is formed. The stalk can be made as tall as an average room. Several stalks put together look like cornstalks. Other possibilities for using this structure may come to mind while it is being made.

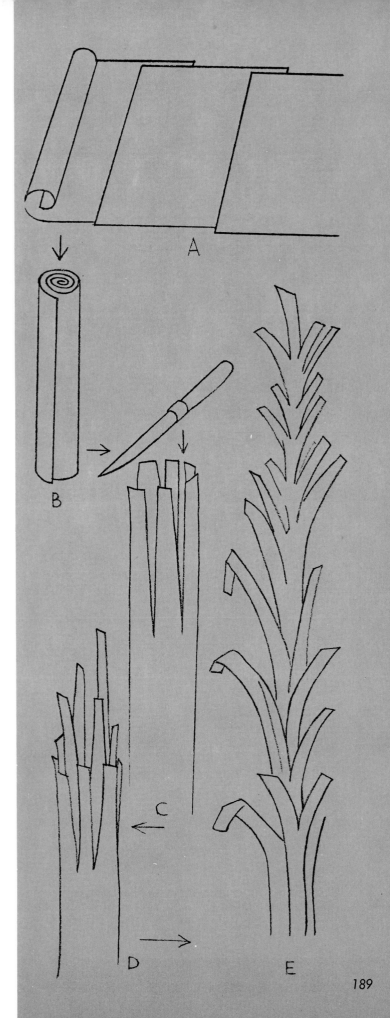

189

STAND-UP CONSTRUCTIONS

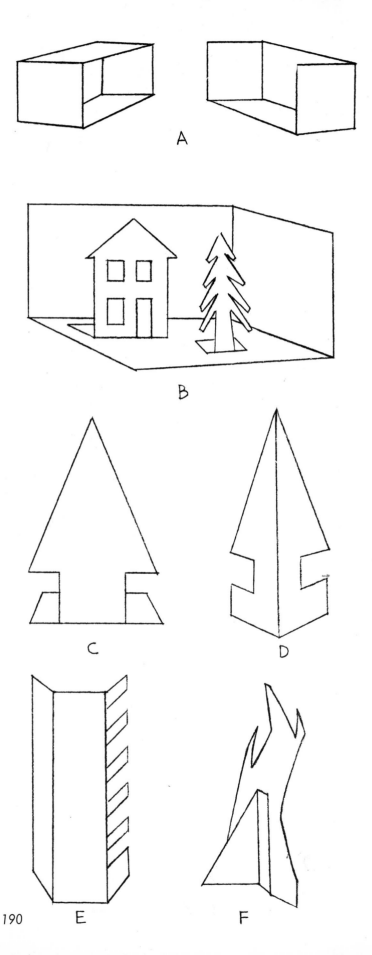

A

B

C

D

E

F

Groupings of small stand-up structures arranged to carry out a theme can be constructed as miniature stage sets, doll houses, dioramas, or shadow boxes. The Nativity, a farm, or a circus are possible subjects to explore.

The photographs at the bottom of this page and the next show stand-up structures created by children. The colonial pulpit is an interpretation of a social studies unit by a child in the fourth grade. The little still-life composition is formed of shapes made three-dimensional by scoring. The jungle scene was made from leftover scraps of colored papers organized within a cardboard carton.

Some of the many ways of making such structures stand up are shown in the diagrams. The structuring of planes on pages 86-87 and the animals on pages 102-5 should also be considered.

The delight of designing, cutting, and shaping furnishings of paper for a favorite doll house can lead to a future interest in the field of interior design. The model shown on the facing page is developed from a cardboard carton modified with corrugated cardboard on the outside. The small structures inside are formed with care and thought, combining paint, colored paper pieces, and patterned areas cut from magazines.

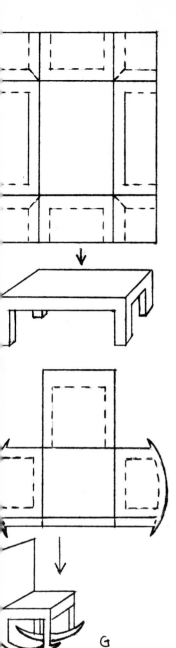

G

BULLETIN

BOARDS

Bulletin boards can be dramatized by the use of papers for attractive displays. A few basic principles, combined with imagination, produce exciting results. The layout of this book is a good example of how space can be organized, and might be a helpful guide in working out bulletin board arrangements. Figure 1 is composed of 5-inch squares of colored Japanese papers supplemented with interesting magazine cutouts. Both positive and negative cutout letters are used. Figure 2 is organized in horizontal-vertical directions emphasized by the arrows. Strong contrasts of dark and light give force to the plan. Figure 3, on the facing page, is composed of three-dimensional shapes combined with flat, decorated papers, based on a checkerboard plan.

1

2

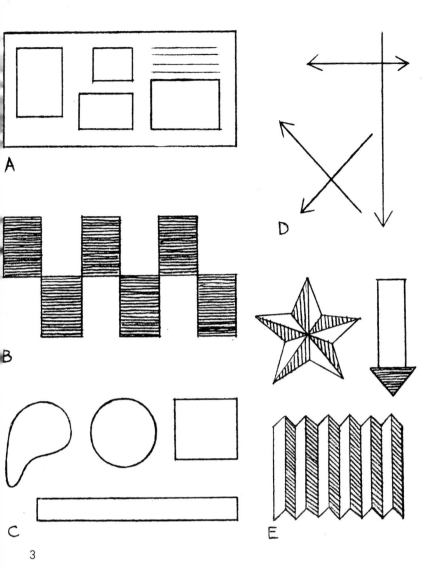

PRINCIPLES OF ARRANGEMENT

A. *Space.* Consider the background area as it relates to the shapes placed against it. Negative and positive shapes should balance one another. It is desirable to keep outside margins lined up.

B. *Rhythm.* This may come from repetition of shape and color, or by parallelism of line movement. The checkerboard plan is a good arrangement. The use of dark and light brings in the necessary contrast.

C. *Shapes.* Think of the display material in terms of definite shapes to be balanced and related. Words are rectangular shapes equal in importance to other shapes.

D. *Direction.* Avoid confusion by limiting the directions of movement. A vertical-horizontal plan is effective for securing unity with dignity and restraint. Diagonals, if used, should be limited in number and direction.

E. *Interest devices.* Use "spot" shapes to attract attention. Pleasing paper forms, string, yarns, and textured papers are available for use.

3

The bulletin board mural at the left, expressing a pioneer theme with paper structured figures, church, and trees, is the work of fourth-grade children. A shelf serves as a support for some of the objects.

The same group of children designed the historical scene with the boat. For this they devised three-dimensional sails, rhythmic waves, and rocks of crushed paper.

CHILDREN'S *ACTIVITIES *

1

2

3

The Thanksgiving bulletin board above was first worked out with butcher paper and later translated into color. Scoring, fringing, and various cuttings and foldings are used to express the pioneer theme. Figure 2 shows the turkey remade of colored papers with decorative spots added to the tail, zigzag folds down the neck, and twisted paper for legs and feet. How much more exciting the result is than the traditional patterns often used.

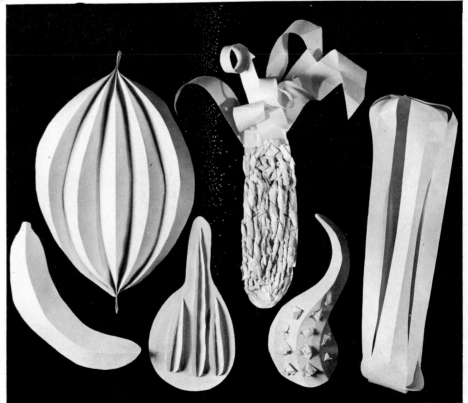

4

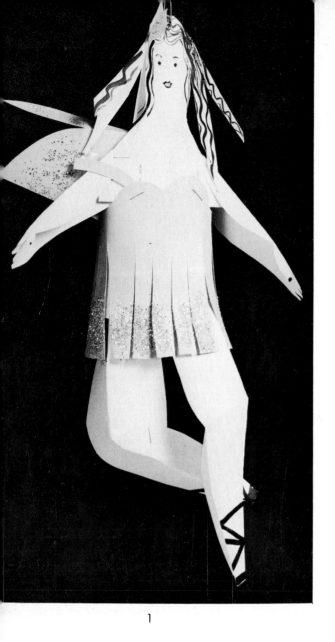

1

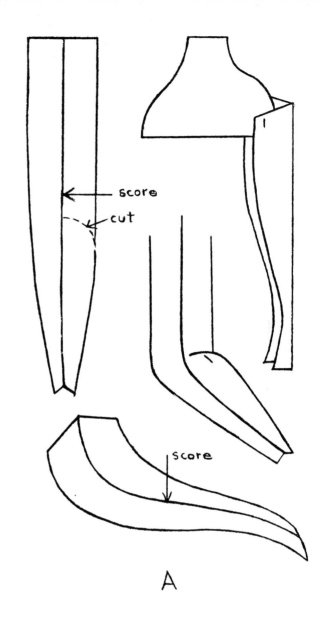

score

cut

score

A

2

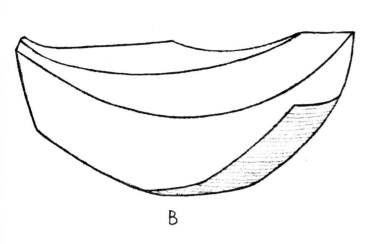

B

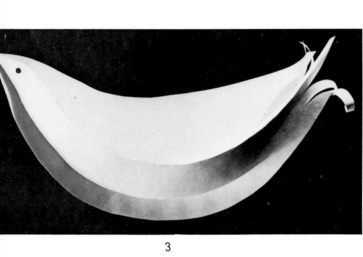

3

4

5

A fascinating yet simple approach to bulletin board design is through the use of scored shapes, which are semiround and can be placed against a flat background. The contours can suggest the subject matter, which can be developed in greater detail with paint and brush. Diagram B shows how a few scored lines permit parts to be bent so that a three-dimensional quality is achieved. Diagram A on the facing page shows some of the separate scored parts that were assembled for figure 1. The bulletin board in figure 2 is an example of good spatial relationships in restrained yet rhythmic movement.

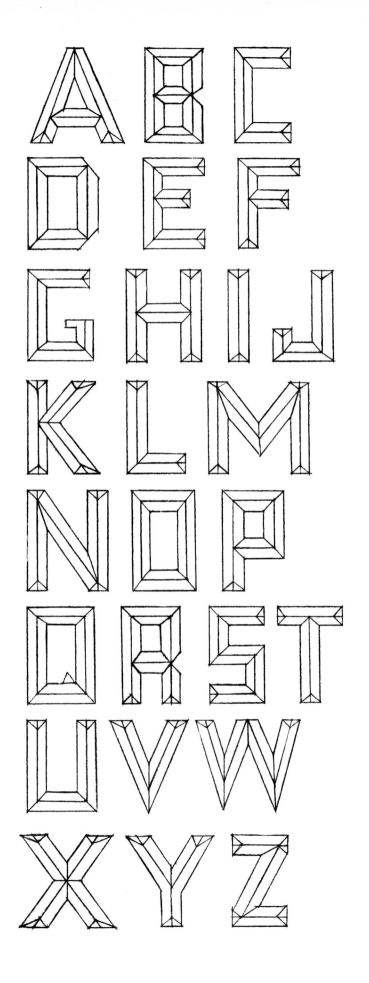

Three-dimensional letters can be used as part of the design of a bulletin board. The letters on this page are made of strips of paper, creased or curved to form the letter shapes. Attached pieces, like the crossbar of the A, can be made with tabs on the ends to paste to the sides. The letters on the facing page are cut out and scored with a dull instrument to give a raised effect. Letters of this type are used on the Thanksgiving bulletin board on page 195.

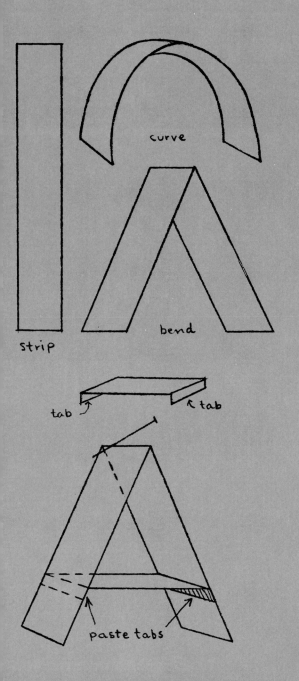

strip

curve

bend

tab

tab

paste tabs

FRAMES

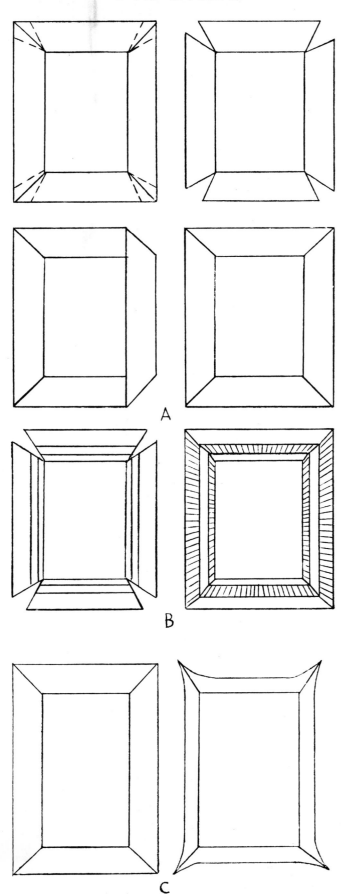

A

B

C

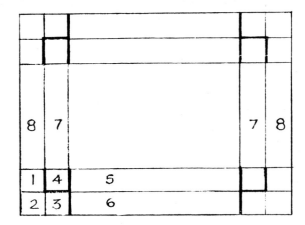

Crease all lines. Cut heavy lines. Fold 5 upward. Fold 4 around 5. Fold 2 and 3 so that 2 is under 1 and 3 is under 6. Use paste to hold. Do the same at the other three corners.

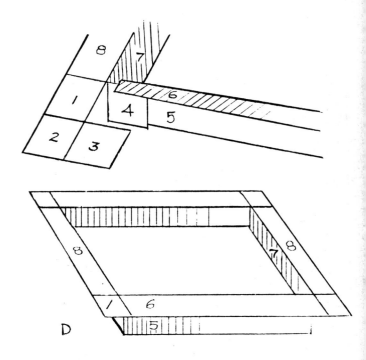

D

Paper frames are effective backgrounds for three-dimensional structures as well as for flat compositions. They can be constructed very simply by cutting out the corners or by pinching them together. In diagram A a triangle shape is cut from each corner and the edges are taped together. This frame can be used either front or back. A frame with several scored and creased lines is shown in diagram B. All lines in diagram C are creased or scored and the corners are pinched together. Another frame is explained in diagram D.

1

When children are permitted freedom to explore and discover some of the potentials of paper, they usually respond with much interest. Without limitations and direction, however, the experience will be wasted, often ending in confusion. The child needs opportunities for developing his imagination and arousing latent sense perceptions in order to realize and make use of the abilities he possesses. Character traits are brought out as self-confidence grows, and under the guidance of a sensitive, sympathetic teacher the child's excitements and discoveries are shared and encouraged. Personal development is affected by the quality of the experience as it brings out the inborn sense of rhythm, develops powers of observation, and encourages a feeling of kinship with the world around. It is for this reason that educators are opposed to giving patterns to be traced or copied. This does not imply neglect or lack of direction, but rather a pointing of the way through stimulation and guided approaches.

2

Trying different approaches to working with paper encourages children to learn something of its various properties. For some kinds of problems, many will find it easier to work directly in the paper with scissors or fingers than to draw first with a pencil. Simple ways of cutting squares and circles without the use of a ruler or compass facilitate creative work. Children can also learn to construct cones and cylinders, to fringe and cut paper, and to work with various other techniques for paper construction, as illustrated in this book. To encourage experimentation and challenge inventive powers, a structure like a pleated rectangle, shown on page 43, can be presented as a point of departure. Maneuvering the shape into different positions suggests new forms and leads to all kinds of creative applications. A number of such possibilities are shown on pages 44 and 45, but it is desirable to let children make their own discoveries and work out their own solutions.

A paper sack stuffed with crushed newspapers and tied or taped at the open end makes a good foundation for constructing animals, birds, or people and helps children to think in terms of three dimensions (see figure 4, page 177). Teachers will find it helpful to keep a box for pieces of paper of various colors to be used for exploring purposes. The examples on this page and the facing one show work done by children using scraps of paper. Figure 1 is woven of strips, with shorter strips woven on top to create the shape of the horse. The horse and rider structure in figure 2 is created of colored paper pieces combined with yarn. The two capricious-looking birds were inspired by a stuffed model from a museum and interpreted with bits of torn papers applied with paste.

3

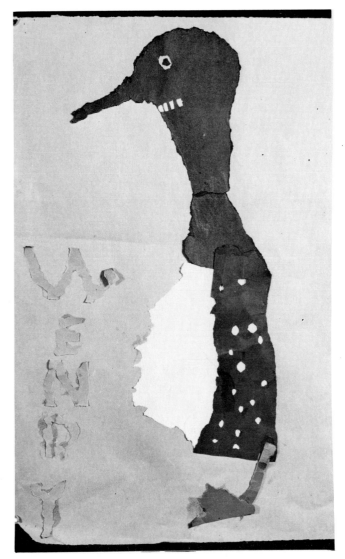

4

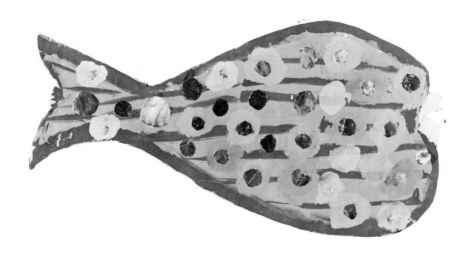

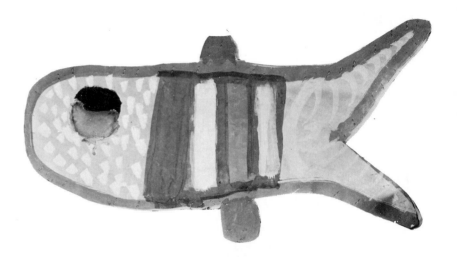

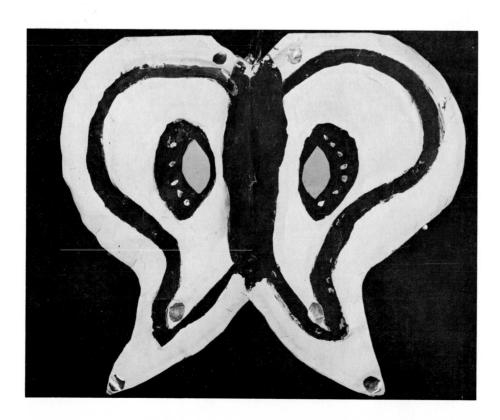

The children working at the easels above are participants in an art class where the environment reflects the productivity of creative experience. Here are found inviting materials and a setting for encouraging all kinds of activities. Easel boards hooked to wire screening, low tables, and adequate floor space for working on large forms all contribute to meeting the needs of these young artists. Mobile creations of double pieces of heavy wrapping paper decorated with paint in vivid colors, like those on the facing page, are suspended from wires above. In such surroundings creativity is stressed in every way possible and the children are exposed to colors and shapes and stimulating forms.

REFERENCES

Adachi, Katsuyuki. *A Japanese Paper-folding Classic*. Washington, D.C.: Pinecone Press, 1961. Excerpt from the "lost" *Kan No Modo*.

Allport, Alan. *Paper Sculpture*. London: Pelham; New York: Drake Publishers, 1971.

American Craftsmen's Council. "Made with Paper" exhibition catalogue. New York: Museum of Contemporary Crafts, 1967.

Angrave, Bruce. *Sculpture in Paper*. London and New York: Studio Publications, 1957.

Aspden, George. *Model Making in Paper, Cardboard, and Metal*. New York: Reinhold Publishers, 1965.

Aurey, Graham, Ben Gates, and Ian Price. *New Ideas in Card and Paper Crafts*. New York: D. Van Nostrand Co., 1973.

Bayer, Herbert, et al., eds. *Bauhaus: 1919-1928*. 1st ed., 1938. Reprint. New York: Museum of Modern Art, 1972.

Grater, Michael. *Make It in Paper: A Simple Introduction to Paper Sculpture for Children, Teachers, and Students*. London: Mills and Boon, 1961.

————. *One Piece of Paper*. London: Mills and Boon, 1963.

————. *Paper People*. New York: Taplinger Publishing Co., 1970.

Honda, Isao. *The World of Origami*. Translated by Richard L. Gage. New York: Japan Publications Trading Co., 1965.

Hughes, Tony. *How to Make Shapes in Space*. New York: E. P. Dutton and Co., 1955.

Iwamiya, Takeji. *Katachi: Japanese Pattern and Design in Wood, Paper, and Clay*. New York: H. N. Abrams, 1963.

Johnston, Mary Grace. *Paper Sculpture* (portfolio). Worcester, Mass.: Davis Press, 1952.

Kasahara, Kunihiko. *Creative Origami*. London: Pitman, 1970.

Krinsky, Norman, and Bill Berry. *Paper Construction for Children*. New York: Reinhold Publishers, 1966.

Lewis, Shari, and Lillian Oppenheimer. *Folding Paper Masks*. New York: E. P. Dutton and Co., 1965.

————. *Folding Paper Puppets*. New York: Stein and Day, 1962.

————. *Folding Paper Toys*. New York: Stein and Day, 1963.

Lipski, Tadeusz. *Paper Sculpture*. New York: Studio Publications, 1947.

Mander, Jerry, George Dippel, and Howard Gossage. *The Great International Paper Airplane Book*. New York: Simon and Schuster, 1967.

Martin, Marie Gilbert. *Pasteless Construction with Paper*. New York: Pageant Press, 1951.

Matisse, Henry. *Papiers Découpés*. Paris: Berggruen et Cie, 1953.

McPharlin, Paul. *Paper Sculpture—Its Construction and Uses for Display and Decoration.* New York: Hastings House, 1944.

Moholy-Nagy, L. *The New Vision.* New York: W. W. Norton Co., 1938.

Moseley, Spencer, Pauline Johnson, and Hazel Koenig. *Crafts Design.* Belmont, Calif.: Wadsworth Publishing Co., 1962.

Murray, William D., and Francis J. Rigney. *Paper Folding for Beginners.* New York: Dover Publications, 1960.

Newman, Thelma, Jay Hartley Newman, and Lee Scott Newman. *Paper as Art and Craft.* New York: Crown Publishers, 1973.

Ogawa, Hiroshi. *Forms of Paper.* New York: Van Nostrand Reinhold Co., 1971.

Ody, Kenneth. *Paper Folding and Paper Sculpture.* New York: Emerson Books, 1965.

Palestraunt, Simon S. *Practical Papercraft.* New York: Homecrafts, 1950.

Payne, G. *Adventures in Paper Modelling.* New York: F. Warne, 1966.

Portchmouth, John. *All Kinds of Papercrafts.* New York: Viking Press, 1972.

Rainey, Sarita, and Arnel W. Pattemore. *Ways with Paper: Construction and Poster.* Worcester, Mass.: Davis Publications, 1971.

Rottger, Ernst. *Creative Paper Design.* New York: Van Nostrand Reinhold Co., 1961.

Rubi, Christian. *Cut Paper, Silhouettes and Stencils: An Instruction Book.* Translated by Alba Lorman. London: Kaye and Ward; New York: Van Nostrand Reinhold Co., 1972.

Sadler, Arthur. *An Introduction to Paper Sculpture.* London: Blanford Press, 1965.
———. *Paper Sculpture.* New York: Pitman Publishing, n.d.

Sakoda, James Minoru. *Modern Origami.* New York: Simon and Schuster, 1969.

Sarasas, Claude. *Folding Paper for Children.* Tokyo: Dainippon Yubenkai Kodasha, 1951.

Seidelman, James E., and Grace Mintonye. *Creating with Paper.* New York: Macmillan, 1967.

Soong, Maying. *The Art of Chinese Paper Folding for Young and Old.* New York: Harcourt Brace and Co., 1948.

Sundara Rao, Tandalam. *Geometric Exercises in Paper Folding.* 2nd ed., 1905. Reprint. New York: Dover Publications, 1966.

Temko, Florence. *Paper Cutting.* New York: Doubleday, 1973.
———. *Paper Folded, Cut, Sculptured.* New York: Collier Macmillan Publishers, 1974.

Teng, Yun-chang (Kung). *The Art of Grandma Teng.* Taipei: China Publishing Co., 1968.

Wood, Louise. *Make It with Paper.* New York: D. McKay Co., 1970.

Yamada, Sadami, and Ito Kiyotada. *New Dimensions in Paper Craft.* Tokyo and Rutland, Vt.: Japan Publications Trading Co., 1966.